# North Country
# CABIN
# COOKING

## 275 Quick & Easy Recipes

Margie Knoblauch and
Mary Brubacher

Adventure Publications
Cambridge, Minnesota

# Dedication

We dedicate this book, with love and gratitude, to those who have generously shared their recipes with us . . . and to our families, the ultimate taste-testers

Cover and book design by Lora Westberg

Edited by Dan Downing and Emily Beaumont

Cover photo: **Jenn Huls/shutterstock.com:** lace; **istetiana/shutterstock.com:** main image; **pandora64/shutterstock.com:** gingham; **RN_PHOTO/shutterstock.com:** back cover background image

Used under license from Shutterstock.com:
**1989studio:** 84; **Africa Studio:** 125; **Anastasia_Panait:** 136-137; **Angorius:** wooden spoon; **Nataliya Arzamasova:** 80-81; **bergamont:** 62; **Binh Thanh Bui:** 65; **Irina Burakova:** 207; **Dream79:** 60-61; **etorres:** 3; **Fanfo:** 58; **Fischer Food Design:** 51, 151; **BW Folsom:** 175; **Thomas Francois:** 72; **Joe Gough:** 40, 120-121; **GrigoryL:** 187; **GSDesign:** 90; **gutsulyak:** 167; **Quang Ho:** 20; **Brent Hofacker:** 6-7; **Lepas:** 100; **matkub2499:** 104; **Vasily Menshov:** 19; **MicrostockStudio:** 133; **Olga Miltsova:** 147; **Sky Motion:** 143; **Nattika:** 67; **Oxie99:** 92; **M. Unal Ozmen:** 182; **nortongo:** 139; **Pixel-Shot:** 70; **Ratana21:** 39; **Passakorn sakulphan:** 27; **Oksana Shufrych:** 184; **Ekaterina Smirnova:** 16-17; **Anton Starikov:** 74; **Sakoodter Stocker:** 108; **Philip Stridh:** 45; **Diana Taliun:** 86, 155; **Tiger Images:** 30; **ANTONIO TRUZZI:** 56; **Tunedin by Westend61:** 189; **Randall Vermillion:** 36-37; **Elena Veselova:** 192-193; **Teri Virbickis:** 46-47; **Hong Vo:** 128; **Yeti Studio:** 24; **Feng Yu:** 148

10 9 8 7 6 5 4 3 2

**North Country Cabin Cooking: 275 Quick and Easy Recipes**
Third Edition 2019
Copyright © 1983, 2011 and 2019
Published by Adventure Publications
An imprint of AdventureKEEN
310 Garfield Street South
Cambridge, Minnesota 55008
(800) 678-7006
www.adventurepublications.net
All rights reserved
Printed in China
ISBN 978-1-59193-926-9 (pbk.), ISBN 978-1-59193-927-6 (ebook)

# Table of Contents

# Introduction

"Going to the cabin" is a common phrase in the Upper Midwest. On weekends and holidays, we "cabin people," looking for a change of pace, flock to the North Country's lakes and forests. Too often, however, we work just as hard cooking at the cabin as we do at home.

We want to be proud of the food we serve, but we want to be "on vacation" too. The recipes we present here are intended to make time spent at the cabin enjoyable for everyone—including the cook. Many of these recipes can be made at home and taken to the cabin. Others are one-dish meals that can be prepared easily in the cabin kitchen. All are geared for the vacationer or weekend "cabin person."

We requested recipes from friends and relatives who have cabins, and from others who understand the need for more casual cooking while vacationing. We asked for recipes that are tasty and popular, can be made in advance and conveniently transported, are easy to prepare, and use ingredients that are readily available—even in small, out-of-the-way grocery stores and markets.

In gathering these recipes, we learned that most of us, when going to the cabin for a short time, prepare food at home and take it with us. By doing so, we can enjoy our leisure time and still have delicious home-cooked meals.

Organization is the key to having that leisure time. Try to plan menus and prepare food in advance whenever possible. Measure and mix dry ingredients for a recipe at home, especially if that recipe requires spices or seasonings not stocked at the cabin. Put the mixture into a plastic bag or other container, and label it accordingly.

Sharing cooking responsibilities also helps ensure leisure time for everyone. When a cabin is being shared by two or more families, each family can be responsible for a meal. Have a group of young people? Use a kaper chart, as the Scouts do, to assign meal-time tasks.

Planning ahead, sharing kitchen duties, and using the recipes presented here should greatly reduce the amount of time spent in cabin kitchens preparing meals.

To those who contributed these recipes, we extend a heartfelt "thank you." To the reader, we express our hopes that this cookbook helps cabin cooks everywhere have more time to relax and enjoy those golden days in the North Country.

# Appetizers & Snacks

# Curry Dip

### INGREDIENTS

1⅓ cups mayonnaise

2 tablespoons honey

2 tablespoons ketchup

2 tablespoons grated onion

Dash of salt

1 tablespoon lemon juice

7 drops Tabasco sauce

1 teaspoon curry powder

### DIRECTIONS

Combine all ingredients in a small serving bowl. Serve with fresh vegetables, such as cauliflower florets and sliced bell peppers, celery, carrots, tomatoes, mushrooms, etc.

# Nacho Dip

### INGREDIENTS

2 (16-ounce) cans refried beans

1 large onion, chopped and sautéed until tender

1 (4-ounce) can diced green chiles, drained

1½ cups mild taco sauce

16 ounces shredded cheddar cheese

16 ounces shredded Monterey Jack cheese

### DIRECTIONS

Preheat oven to 325°.

Layer all ingredients (in order) in a 9x13-inch pan.

Bake for 25 minutes. Serve with tortilla chips, crackers, etc.

# Baked Cheese Dip

## INGREDIENTS

1 cup mayonnaise (not low-fat)

1 cup shredded sharp cheddar cheese

1 medium onion, minced or grated

Paprika or parsley (optional)

## DIRECTIONS

Preheat oven to 400°.

Combine mayonnaise, cheese, and onion in a shallow baking dish or 9-inch pie plate. Sprinkle with paprika or parsley, if desired, for color.

Bake 15–20 minutes or until lightly browned. Serve with crackers or fresh vegetables.

 **Note:** This recipe may be doubled for a large group.

# Rye and Dip

*Make the dip at home and take it with you. Prepare the bread just before serving.*

## INGREDIENTS

1 (1-pound) loaf unsliced rye bread

⅔ cup sour cream

⅔ cup mayonnaise

1 teaspoon dried dill weed or dill seed

1 teaspoon Beau Monde seasoning

1 tablespoon onion flakes

1 tablespoon dried parsley

## DIRECTIONS

Cut an oval or rectangular hole in top of bread, leaving at least 1 inch of bread at the bottom of the loaf. Remove cut section; break into bite-size chunks. Place hollowed-out loaf and bread chunks back in bread bag until ready to use.

Combine sour cream and next 5 ingredients in an airtight container. Refrigerate dip overnight.

To serve, fill loaf with dip and surround with bread chunks for dipping. (You may want to double this popular dip recipe.)

# Dip for Raw Vegetables

## INGREDIENTS

2 cups sour cream (or 1 cup sour cream plus 1 cup mayonnaise)

1 package (1.5–2 ounces, depending on brand) vegetable soup and dip mix

¼ teaspoon curry powder (optional)

## DIRECTIONS

Combine sour cream, soup mix, and, if desired, curry powder in a serving bowl.

Refrigerate at least 1 hour. Serve with fresh vegetables or chips.


# Chopped Vegetable Spread

## INGREDIENTS

1 cup finely chopped celery

1 green bell pepper, finely chopped

1 small onion, minced

1 large cucumber, finely chopped

1 (0.25-ounce) package unflavored gelatin mix

2 cups mayonnaise

1 teaspoon salt

## DIRECTIONS

Place celery, bell pepper, onion, and cucumber in a serving bowl; drain juices, if necessary. Mix gelatin with ¼ cup cold water in a saucepan. Add ¼ cup boiling water. Stir in mayonnaise and salt. Stir mixture into vegetables. Chill. Serve with crackers such as Wheat Thins.

 **Note:** A food processor comes in handy for making this recipe.

# Quick Shrimp Spread

## INGREDIENTS

1 (8-ounce) package cream cheese, softened

1 (12-ounce) bottle Heinz chili sauce

2 (4-ounce) cans tiny shrimp, rinsed and drained

## DIRECTIONS

Spread cream cheese on a shallow dish or small platter. Cover with chili sauce (you may not need the entire bottle). Top with shrimp. Serve with crackers.

# Cheese Balls

## INGREDIENTS

1 (8-ounce) package cream cheese, softened

1 (4-ounce) jar diced pimientos, drained

1 (4-ounce) package smoked cheddar cheese, shredded

½ cup butter, softened

2 tablespoons minced onion

1 tablespoon Worcestershire sauce

½ teaspoon salt

¼ teaspoon garlic powder

Chopped roasted nuts or parsley

## DIRECTIONS

Combine cream cheese and next 7 ingredients in a large bowl using an electric mixer. Form mixture into 3 balls. Roll each in chopped nuts or parsley. Chill in refrigerator until firm. Wrap and freeze, if desired. Serve with crackers.

# Hot Triscuit Hors d'Oeuvres

### INGREDIENTS

4 ounces shredded mozzarella cheese

4 ounces shredded cheddar cheese

½ (6-ounce) can black olives, drained and chopped

6 green onions (with tops), finely chopped

½ cup mayonnaise

Triscuits

### DIRECTIONS

Preheat oven to 375°.

Combine cheeses, olives, onion, and mayonnaise in a bowl. Spread cheese mixture on Triscuits, and place on a baking sheet.

Bake for 7 minutes.

# Howie's Dill Pickle Special

### INGREDIENTS

1 jar whole dill pickles

1 (2.5-ounce) jar dried beef

1 (8-ounce) package cream cheese, softened

### DIRECTIONS

Drain pickles, and pat dry with paper towels. Spread one side of each slice of dried beef with cream cheese, covering completely.

Place a pickle in the center of each prepared beef slice, with the cream cheese side up; roll beef slice around pickle. Insert toothpicks through each pickle at ½-inch intervals. Slice wrapped pickles into ½-inch rounds.

Cover and refrigerate until ready to serve.

# Taco Dip Hors d'Oeuvres

## INGREDIENTS

1 (8-ounce) package cream cheese, softened

1 (8-ounce) container sour cream

⅛ teaspoon garlic salt

Shredded iceberg lettuce (about ½ a head)

⅔ cup finely chopped onion

¼ cup finely chopped green bell pepper

2 medium tomatoes, seeded and finely chopped

1 cup shredded cheddar cheese

1 tablespoon chopped black olives

Taco sauce

## DIRECTIONS

Combine cream cheese, sour cream, and garlic salt in a small bowl. Mix well. Spread mixture on a shallow plate. Chill in refrigerator for 15 minutes.

Sprinkle lettuce, onion, bell pepper, tomatoes, cheddar cheese, and olives over cream cheese mixture. Dot with taco sauce just before serving. Serve with tortilla chips for dipping.

 **Note:** This can be prepared early in the day.

# Mini-Pizza

## INGREDIENTS

Ritz or Triscuit crackers

Mozzarella cheese slices, cut into quarters

Pizza or marinara sauce

Pepperoni slices

## DIRECTIONS

Preheat oven to 350°.

Place crackers on a baking sheet. Layer with cheese, sauce, and pepperoni.

Bake 3–5 minutes.

# Dill Squares

*Prepare the cheese spread at home. Refrigerate until needed at your destination, and then allow the mixture to soften before spreading.*

### INGREDIENTS

½ cup butter, softened

¼ teaspoon Tabasco sauce

¼ teaspoon Worcestershire sauce

¼ teaspoon onion powder

2 teaspoons dried dill weed

Dash of cayenne pepper

1 (5-ounce) jar Old English cheese spread

1 loaf Pepperidge Farm Very Thin white bread

### DIRECTIONS

Preheat oven to 350°.

Combine butter and next 5 ingredients in a large bowl using an electric mixer. Add cheese spread and mix well. Spread each slice of bread with butter-cheese mixture. Stack two slices of bread together, both with the cheese side up. Trim crusts from "sandwich," and cut each into 6 squares. Repeat with remaining prepared bread slices. Sandwiches must be cut before baking. Place sandwich squares on a baking sheet.

Bake for 15 minutes or until browned.

# North Country Seafood Cocktail

*This is a great way to use leftover cooked fish—sunnies, crappies, bluegills, northerns, or walleyes.*

### INGREDIENTS

Cooked fish

Cocktail sauce

Shredded lettuce (optional)

### GARNISH

Lemon slices

### DIRECTIONS

Break fish into bite-size pieces, discarding skin and bones; place fish in a large bowl. Gently stir in cocktail sauce to coat. Serve individually in cups or small glasses. Or place shredded lettuce on a serving platter, top with coated fish pieces, and garnish with lemon slices, if desired.

# Bite-Size Stuffies

## INGREDIENTS

1 loaf frozen bread dough, thawed overnight in refrigerator

36 stuffed green olives or cubes of ham, cheese, or cooked shrimp

Butter

## DIRECTIONS

Preheat oven to 400°.

Using scissors, cut thawed dough into 36 pieces. Shape each dough piece around 1 olive or piece of ham, cheese, or shrimp. Seal edges well. Place on a lightly greased baking sheet. Cover and let rise until puffy (about 30 minutes).

Bake 10–12 minutes. Brush with melted butter.

 **Note:** To prepare in the morning and bake later in the day, store stuffed bread pieces on a lightly greased baking sheet in the refrigerator until ready to let rise (at room temperature for at least 30 minutes before baking).

# Gorp

## INGREDIENTS

Raisins

Dry roasted peanuts

Sunflower seeds, shelled

Slivered almonds

Choice of one of the following: M&M's, Reese's Pieces, carob chips, or chocolate chips

## DIRECTIONS

Mix together equal amounts of all ingredients in a large airtight container or plastic bag.

# Breads & Breakfast

# Susie's Simple Beer Bread

**INGREDIENTS**

3 cups self-rising flour

1 can of beer, at room temperature

4 tablespoons sugar

**DIRECTIONS**

Preheat oven to 350°.

Combine all ingredients in a large bowl. Mix well. Pour batter into a greased bread pan.

Bake for 45 minutes.

Makes 2 loaves or 4 mini-loaves.

# Prairie Brown Bread

**INGREDIENTS**

4 cups whole-wheat flour

1⅓ cups all-purpose flour

1 quart buttermilk

2 cups brown sugar

4 teaspoons baking soda

1 teaspoon salt

**DIRECTIONS**

Preheat oven to 350°.

Combine all ingredients in a large bowl. Pour batter into 2 greased bread pans (or 4 mini-loaf pans).

Bake for 1 hour. (If baking mini-loaves, check after 40 minutes.) Remove from pans to cool on a wire rack.

Makes 1 loaf.

# Strawberry Bread

## INGREDIENTS

3 cups all-purpose flour

2 cups sugar

1 teaspoon baking soda

1½ teaspoons cinnamon

1 teaspoon salt

1 (3-ounce) package strawberry
gelatin mix

4 eggs, beaten

1 (16-ounce) package frozen
strawberries, thawed

1¼ cups butter, softened

1¼ cups chopped walnuts

## DIRECTIONS

Preheat oven to 350°.

Combine flour, sugar, baking soda, cinnamon, salt,
and gelatin mix in a large bowl. Make a well in center
of mixture. Stir together eggs, strawberries, butter, and
walnuts in a small bowl; pour egg mixture into well
and stir by hand. Pour batter into 5 greased and floured
mini-loaf pans (3x5-inch size).

Bake for about 40 minutes or until a toothpick inserted
in center comes out clean.

Makes 5 mini-loaves.

# Banana Blueberry Bread

## INGREDIENTS

3 cups all-purpose flour

1½ cups sugar

4 teaspoons baking powder

1 teaspoon salt

1½ cups quick-cooking oats

⅔ cup vegetable oil

4 eggs, slightly beaten

2 cups mashed very ripe banana

2 cups fresh or frozen blueberries,
rinsed, drained, and patted dry
with paper towels

## DIRECTIONS

Preheat oven to 350°.

Combine flour, sugar, baking powder, and salt in a large
bowl. Stir in oats. Add oil, eggs, and banana, stirring just
until mixed. Gently fold in blueberries. Pour batter into
2 greased 4x8-inch loaf pans.

Bake 50–60 minutes or until a toothpick inserted in
center comes out clean. Let cool in pans for 10 minutes,
then remove from pans to a wire rack. When cool, wrap
in foil and refrigerate for several hours before slicing.

Makes 2 loaves.

# Monkey Bread

## INGREDIENTS

4 (7.5-ounce) packages refrigerated buttermilk biscuits

1 cup granulated sugar

1 teaspoon cinnamon

1 cup brown sugar

¾ cup butter

## DIRECTIONS

Preheat oven to 350°.

Using scissors, cut each biscuit into quarters. Mix granulated sugar and cinnamon together in a small bowl. Dip biscuit pieces in sugar mixture to coat. Layer biscuit pieces in a well-greased Bundt pan.

Melt brown sugar and butter in a saucepan over medium heat. Do not boil. Pour over biscuit pieces in pan.

Bake for about 30 minutes. Let cool for 10 minutes, and then invert onto a plate. Tear off pieces, or cut into slices.

Makes 1 loaf.

# Very Lemon Bread

## INGREDIENTS

½ cup shortening

1¼ cups sugar, divided

Zest of 1 lemon

2 eggs

1½ cups all-purpose flour

1 teaspoon baking powder

¾ teaspoon salt

½ cup milk

Juice of 1 lemon

## DIRECTIONS

Preheat oven to 350°.

Cream shortening and 1 cup sugar in a large bowl using an electric mixer. Add lemon zest. Beat in eggs. In a separate bowl, sift together flour, baking powder, and salt. Add flour mixture to creamed mixture, alternating with milk and stirring just until combined. Pour batter into a 9x5-inch loaf pan.

Bake 50–60 minutes or until a toothpick inserted in center comes out clean. Remove from pan while warm. Prick the top of the loaf with a fork. Mix together remaining ¼ cup sugar and lemon juice; pour over loaf.

Makes 1 loaf.

# Blue Cheese Bread

## INGREDIENTS

½ cup butter, softened

¼ cup crumbled blue cheese

¼ teaspoon salt

⅛ teaspoon pepper

1 loaf French bread, sliced into
  1-inch-thick slices

## DIRECTIONS

Preheat oven to 400°.

Combine butter, cheese, salt, and pepper in a small bowl; spread on each slice of bread slices. Reassemble slices into a "loaf" and wrap in aluminum foil.

Bake for 20 minutes. Serve hot.

Makes 1 loaf.


# Swedish Hardtack

## INGREDIENTS

¾ cup butter

½ cup sugar

2 cups cracked wheat or instant oatmeal

3 cups all-purpose flour

1 teaspoon baking soda

1 teaspoon salt

1½ cups buttermilk

## DIRECTIONS

Cream butter and sugar in a large bowl using an electric mixer. In a separate bowl, combine cracked wheat, flour, baking soda, and salt. Add wheat mixture to creamed mixture, alternating with buttermilk. Form dough into balls (the size of small baseballs). Cover and let rest for about 1 hour. Preheat oven to 375°.

Roll dough balls thin, as for piecrust; place on baking sheets. Bake for about 15 minutes. Watch closely; remove from oven when biscuits begin to brown. When cool, break into pieces and store in an airtight container.

Makes 20 servings.

# Whipped Cream Biscuits

**INGREDIENTS**

1 cup whipping cream

1¼ cups self-rising flour

**DIRECTIONS**

Preheat oven to 375°.

Whip cream in a large bowl, using an electric mixer, until soft peaks form. Mix in flour. Drop dough by tablespoonfuls onto an ungreased baking sheet.

Bake for about 10 minutes or until lightly browned.

# Scandia Valley Skillet Biscuits

**INGREDIENTS**

1 cup buttermilk

¼ teaspoon baking soda

1¾ cups all-purpose flour

1 tablespoon baking powder

½ teaspoon salt

2 tablespoons butter

**DIRECTIONS**

Preheat oven to 450°.

In a large bowl, stir together buttermilk and baking soda. In a separate bowl, combine flour, baking powder, and salt, mixing well. Add flour mixture to buttermilk mixture; stir only until moistened and mixed.

Knead dough on floured board about 15 times. Press dough to 1-inch thickness, and cut with a floured biscuit cutter.

Melt butter in an 8-inch cast iron skillet. Pour off and reserve some of the melted butter, leaving enough butter in the skillet to coat the bottom. Place biscuits in skillet, and drizzle remaining butter over top of biscuits.

Bake 12–15 minutes or until biscuits are medium brown. Serve hot.

Makes 8 biscuits.

# Thumbprint Pastries

## INGREDIENTS

½ cup sugar

1 teaspoon cinnamon

1 (16.3-ounce) can refrigerated big
flaky biscuits

¼ cup butter, melted

Jam or preserves (jelly is too thin)

2 tablespoons butter

## DIRECTIONS

Preheat oven to 350°.

Combine sugar and cinnamon in a small bowl. Dip both sides of each biscuit into melted butter, then in cinnamon-sugar mixture. Make a deep thumbprint in center of each biscuit. Fill with 1–2 teaspoons jam. Place on an ungreased baking sheet.

Bake 13–18 minutes or until golden brown.

Makes 8 pastries.

# Sour Cream Coffee Ring

## BATTER

½ cup butter

1 cup granulated sugar

2 eggs

1 cup sour cream

1 teaspoon vanilla extract

2 cups all-purpose flour

1 teaspoon baking soda

1 teaspoon baking powder

1 teaspoon salt

¼ cup brown sugar

## TOPPING

½ cup chopped nuts

½ cup brown sugar

2 teaspoons cinnamon

## DIRECTIONS

Preheat oven to 350°.

To make batter, cream butter and granulated sugar in a large bowl, using an electric mixer. Beat in eggs. Add sour cream, vanilla, flour, baking soda, baking powder, salt, and ¼ cup brown sugar; mix just until combined.

To make topping, mix together nuts, ½ cup brown sugar, and cinnamon in a small bowl. Pour half of the batter into a greased 10-inch tube pan. Sprinkle with half of the topping. Repeat with remaining batter and topping.

Bake 45–50 minutes or until a toothpick inserted in center comes out clean.

Makes 1 coffee ring.

# Swedish Kringler Coffee Cake

## CRUSTS

½ cup butter

1 cup all-purpose flour

1–2 tablespoons water

## FILLING

1 cup water

½ cup butter

1 cup all-purpose flour

3 eggs

1 teaspoon almond extract

## ICING

1 cup powdered sugar, sifted

1½ tablespoons whipping cream

1 tablespoon butter, softened

2 teaspoons almond extract

Sliced almonds

## DIRECTIONS

Preheat oven to 375°.

To make crusts, cut ½ cup butter into 1 cup flour with a pastry blender in a large bowl; add enough water for dough to come together into a ball. On a baking sheet, press dough into 2 (4-inch-wide) strips the length of the pan.

To make filling, bring 1 cup water and ½ cup butter to a boil in a saucepan. Remove from heat. Stir in 1 cup flour, beating until smooth. Add eggs, one at a time, beating until smooth after each addition. Add 1 teaspoon almond extract. Spread filling over crusts.

Bake for 45 minutes, or until top is crisp and brown.

To make icing, stir together powdered sugar, cream, 1 tablespoon butter, and 2 teaspoons almond extract. Spread on top of cakes. Sprinkle with sliced almonds.

Makes 2 pastries.

# Banana Muffins

## INGREDIENTS

2 cups sugar

½ cup shortening

2 tablespoons vegetable oil

2 cups very ripe mashed banana

3 eggs

2¼ cups cake flour

2½ teaspoons baking soda

2½ teaspoons baking powder

¾ teaspoon salt

¾ teaspoon vanilla extract

1½ teaspoons lemon juice

1 cup buttermilk

## DIRECTIONS

Preheat oven to 375°.

Cream sugar, shortening, and oil in a large bowl using an electric mixer. Add banana and mix well. Add eggs and mix well. In a separate large bowl, combine flour, baking soda, baking powder, and salt. Add flour mixture to creamed mixture. Stir in vanilla and lemon juice. Mix well at low speed. Gradually add buttermilk until smooth. Mix at medium speed for 3 minutes.

Place muffin cup liners in muffin pans; lightly grease with cooking spray. Spoon batter into prepared cups, filling ¾ full.

Bake 20–22 minutes.

Makes 2 dozen.

 **Note:** These freeze well, so you can make them ahead and take them along.

# Big Pine French Toast

## INGREDIENTS

2 cups milk

4 eggs, well beaten

½ teaspoon salt

2 teaspoons cinnamon (optional)

Bread slices

## DIRECTIONS

Whisk together milk, eggs, salt, and, if desired, cinnamon in a large bowl. Dip bread slices into egg mixture until well coated.

Fry slices on an oiled griddle or skillet until golden brown on both sides.

Makes 16 slices.


# Blueberry Muffins

## INGREDIENTS

½ cup butter

1½ cups sugar

2 eggs

½ cup milk

2 cups all-purpose flour

2 teaspoons baking powder

½ teaspoon salt

2 cups fresh or frozen blueberries, rinsed, drained, and patted dry with paper towels

Sugar for sprinkling

## DIRECTIONS

Preheat oven to 375°.

Using a spoon (not a mixer), cream butter and sugar in a large bowl; stir in eggs and milk. In a separate bowl, combine flour, baking powder, and salt. Add flour mixture to creamed mixture. Gently fold blueberries into batter.

Place muffin cup liners in muffin pans; lightly grease with cooking spray. Spoon batter into prepared cups, filling ¾ full. Sprinkle each muffin with a teaspoon of sugar.

Bake 25–30 minutes.

Makes 16 muffins.

 **Note:** These freeze well.

# Breakfast Muffins

## BATTER

⅓ cup butter

½ cup sugar

1 egg

1½ cups all-purpose flour

1½ teaspoons baking powder

½ teaspoon salt

¼ teaspoon nutmeg

½ cup milk

## TOPPING

½ cup sugar

1 teaspoon cinnamon

½ cup butter, melted

## DIRECTIONS

Preheat oven to 350°.

To make batter, cream ⅓ cup butter, ½ cup sugar, and egg in a large bowl using an electric mixer. In a separate large bowl, combine flour, baking powder, salt, and nutmeg. Add flour mixture, alternately with milk, to creamed mixture, being careful not to overmix.

Place 12 muffin cup liners in a muffin pan; lightly grease with cooking spray. Spoon batter into prepared cups, filling ¾ full.

Bake 20–25 minutes.

To make topping, combine ½ cup sugar and cinnamon. Immediately after baking, roll tops of hot muffins in melted ½ cup butter, then dip in cinnamon-sugar mixture. Serve hot.

Makes 1 dozen.

# Bran Muffins

## INGREDIENTS

1 (13.7-ounce) package Raisin Bran cereal

5¼ cups all-purpose flour

5 teaspoons baking soda

2 teaspoons salt

3 cups sugar

½ cup vegetable oil

½ cup butter, melted and cooled

1 quart buttermilk, at room temperature

4 eggs, lightly beaten

1 cup nuts, chopped

1 cup raisins or dates

## DIRECTIONS

Preheat oven to 350°.

In a 4-quart bowl, combine cereal, flour, baking soda, salt, and sugar. In a separate large bowl, mix together oil, butter, buttermilk, eggs, nuts, and raisins. Stir eggs mixture into cereal mixture. (If making ahead, cover lightly; store in refrigerator and use as needed.)

For each dozen, place 12 muffin cup liners in a muffin pan; lightly grease with cooking spray. Spoon batter into prepared cups, filling ¾ full.

Bake for 20 minutes.

Makes 6 dozen.

 **Note:** Batter can be stored in the refrigerator up to 6 weeks.

# Pumpkin Raisin Muffins

### BATTER

1 (30-ounce) can pumpkin pie mix

2 (15.4-ounce) packages nut quick bread and muffin mix

1 egg, beaten

1 cup raisins

### TOPPING

2 tablespoons sugar

1 teaspoon cinnamon

### DIRECTIONS

Preheat oven to 375°.

To make batter, combine pumpkin pie mix, nut bread mix, and egg in a large bowl. Mix just until bread mix is moistened. Stir in raisins. Place muffin cup liners in muffin pans; lightly grease with cooking spray. Spoon batter into prepared cups, filling ¾ full.

To make topping, combine sugar and cinnamon in a small bowl. Sprinkle on top of muffins.

Bake 15–20 minutes or until golden brown.

Makes 30 muffins.

 **Note:** These freeze well.

# Toasty Nut Granola

### INGREDIENTS

6 cups old-fashioned oatmeal, uncooked

½ cup brown sugar

¾ cup wheat germ

½ cup shredded coconut

⅓ cup sesame seeds

1 cup chopped nuts

½ cup vegetable oil

⅓ cup honey

1½ teaspoons vanilla extract

Raisins (optional)

### DIRECTIONS

Preheat oven to 350°.

Place oatmeal in an ungreased 9x13-inch baking dish; bake for 10 minutes. Transfer heated oatmeal to a large bowl, and mix in brown sugar, wheat germ, coconut, sesame seeds, and chopped nuts.

Combine vegetable oil, honey, and vanilla. Stir honey mixture into oatmeal mixture to coat. Divide granola equally between 2 (9x13-inch) baking dishes.

Bake for 20 minutes, stirring often to brown evenly. Cool. Stir in raisins, if desired. Store in tightly covered containers.

Makes 12 servings.

# Apple-Oatmeal Baked Breakfast

## INGREDIENTS

2 cups milk

3 tablespoons brown sugar, divided

1 tablespoon butter

¼ teaspoon salt

¼ teaspoon cinnamon

1 cup old-fashioned oatmeal, uncooked

1 cup peeled and diced apple

½ cup raisins

Milk or cream

## DIRECTIONS

Preheat oven to 350°.

Combine milk, 2 tablespoons brown sugar, butter, salt, and cinnamon in a medium saucepan; scald. Stir in oats, apple, and raisins. Heat, stirring occasionally, until bubbles appear at edge of saucepan. Spoon into a greased 1½-quart baking dish.

Bake for 30 minutes. Halfway through baking, swirl in remaining 1 tablespoon brown sugar. Serve with milk or cream.

Makes 3 servings.

# Puffy French Toast

## INGREDIENTS

1 cup all-purpose flour

1½ teaspoons sugar

1½ teaspoons baking powder

½ teaspoon salt

¼ teaspoon cinnamon

1 cup milk

2 eggs, beaten

8–10 slices bread

Vegetable oil for deep frying

## DIRECTIONS

Sift together flour, sugar, baking powder, salt, and cinnamon in a large bowl. In a separate bowl, combine milk and eggs. Add milk mixture to flour mixture. Beat until smooth. Dip bread slices into batter, turning to coat both sides evenly.

Fry in preheated deep oil (375°) until golden brown, about 2 minutes on each side. Drain.
Serve hot.

Makes 8–10 slices.

# Frozen Orange French Toast

## INGREDIENTS

2 eggs, beaten

1 cup orange juice

1 tablespoon sugar

¼ teaspoon salt

12 slices French bread

6 tablespoons butter

## TOPPINGS

Syrup, butter

## DIRECTIONS

*Advance preparation:* Combine eggs, orange juice, sugar, and salt in a large bowl. Dip bread slices into egg mixture, coating both sides. Place slices on baking sheets. Freeze until firm. Seal slices in an airtight container, and return to freezer.

*Before serving:* Preheat oven to 500°. Place bread slices in a well-buttered, shallow baking dish. Melt 6 tablespoons butter, and drizzle over bread.

Bake for 5 minutes. Turn slices over, and bake about 5 minutes more.

Makes 6 servings.

# Hootenanny Pancakes

## INGREDIENTS

½ cup butter

6 eggs

1 cup milk

1 cup all-purpose flour

½ teaspoon salt

## TOPPINGS

Syrup, jam, powdered sugar, cinnamon-sugar, thinly sliced apples

## DIRECTIONS

Preheat oven to 425°.

Melt butter in a 9x13-inch glass baking dish in the oven; tip pan to coat. Lightly beat eggs and milk together in a large bowl. In a separate bowl, combine flour and salt. Add flour mixture to egg mixture; do not overbeat. Pour batter into prepared pan.

Bake 25–30 minutes. Serve with desired toppings.

Makes 6 servings.

# Make-Ahead Pancake Mix

## PANCAKE MIX

10 cups all-purpose flour

2 cups powdered milk

6 tablespoons baking powder

1½ tablespoons salt

1½ teaspoons cream of tartar

¼ cup sugar

2 cups shortening

## DIRECTIONS

To make mix, sift flour, powdered milk, baking powder, salt, cream of tartar, and sugar together 3 times. Cut shortening into flour mixture. Store in an airtight container.

Makes 40 servings.

*Pancakes for 4:* Beat together 1 cup water and 1 egg in a large bowl. Add 1½ cups Make-Ahead Pancake Mix. Cook batter on a hot griddle.


# Crisp Waffles

## INGREDIENTS

2 eggs, separated

1 cup all-purpose flour

1 cup milk

½ teaspoon salt

1 teaspoon sugar

2 tablespoons vegetable oil

2 tablespoons melted butter

4 teaspoons baking powder

## DIRECTIONS

Combine egg yolks, flour, milk, salt, sugar, oil, and melted butter in a large bowl. In a separate bowl, beat egg whites until stiff but not dry. Add egg whites to flour mixture. Just before baking, fold in baking powder.

Bake in a preheated waffle iron.

Makes 4 waffles, depending on size of waffle iron.

 **Note:** This batter works especially well for thick, Belgian-style waffles.

# German Pancake

## INGREDIENTS

4 tablespoons (½ stick) butter

1 cup all-purpose flour

1 cup milk

4 eggs

Dash of salt

Powdered sugar (optional)

## TOPPINGS

Jam, syrup, or warm applesauce, or sour
   cream and fresh berries

## DIRECTIONS

Preheat oven to 425°.

Melt butter in a 10-inch cast iron skillet in the oven.
Add flour, milk, eggs, and salt to melted butter. Stir
for 45 seconds. Batter will remain somewhat lumpy.

Bake 12–15 minutes. Sprinkle with powdered sugar,
if desired, and serve with desired toppings. Serve
with sausage or bacon.

Makes 4 servings.

 **Note:** Bring this to the table in the skillet!

# Finnish Oven Pancakes

## INGREDIENTS

4 eggs

4 cups milk

2 cups all-purpose flour

¼ teaspoon salt

1 teaspoon sugar

2 tablespoons butter

## TOPPINGS

Syrup, jam

## DIRECTIONS

Preheat oven to 450°.

Combine eggs, milk, flour, salt, and sugar in a large bowl.
Melt 1 tablespoon butter in each of 2 (9x13-inch) baking
dishes in the oven; tip pans to coat with butter. Divide
batter between prepared pans.

Bake about 20–30 minutes or until edges are crispy
brown and top is golden and bubbly. Serve at once
with desired toppings.

Makes 6 servings.

# Eggs & Cheese

# Egg and Cheese Brunch

*Put this together 24 hours before it will be served.*

### INGREDIENTS

Butter

8 slices bread, crusts removed, cubed

1 pound grated sharp cheddar cheese

1 cup diced ham

6 eggs

1½ cups half-and-half

½ teaspoon dry mustard

½ teaspoon salt

### DIRECTIONS

Butter a 9x13-inch baking dish. Place bread cubes in bottom of dish. Cover with cheese and ham. Combine eggs, half-and-half, dry mustard, and salt in a large bowl; pour egg mixture over top.

Cover and refrigerate 24 hours. Remove from refrigerator 2 hours before baking.

Bake, uncovered, at 325° for 1½ hours.

Makes 8 servings.

# Company-at-the-Cabin Brunch

### INGREDIENTS

18 eggs

1 cup plus 2 tablespoons half-and-half

3 tablespoons butter

1 (10.5-ounce) can cream of mushroom soup

1 (4-ounce) can or 1 (6-ounce) jar sliced mushrooms, drained

5 ounces (about 1¼ cups) shredded cheddar cheese

3–4 slices bacon, cooked and crumbled

### DIRECTIONS

Preheat oven to 250°.

Beat eggs and half-and-half together in a large bowl. Melt butter in a large skillet over medium heat. Add egg mixture, and scramble lightly. Transfer eggs to a large, shallow baking dish. Spread soup over eggs; sprinkle mushrooms and cheese over top. Top with bacon.

Bake 45–60 minutes.

Makes 10–12 servings

 **Note:** This can be prepared the night before and refrigerated overnight; increase baking time to 1½ hours.

# Lake Country Eggs and Sausage

*Prepare this recipe the night before.*

## INGREDIENTS

4 slices white bread, cubed

1 cup shredded sharp cheddar cheese

¾ pound breakfast bulk sausage, cooked and drained

4 eggs, beaten

1½ cups milk, divided

¼ teaspoon dry mustard

½ (10.5-ounce) can cream of mushroom soup

## DIRECTIONS

Layer bread, cheese, and sausage in a lightly greased 8x8-inch baking dish. Combine eggs, 1¼ cups milk, and dry mustard in a small bowl; pour over top.

Cover and refrigerate overnight.

Preheat oven to 300°.

Combine soup and ¼ cup milk in a small bowl. Pour over top of casserole.

Bake, uncovered, for 1½ hours.

Makes 4 servings.

**Note:** A double recipe can be made in a 9x13-inch pan.

# Fluffy Oven Eggs and Bacon

## INGREDIENTS

½ pound bacon (about 12 slices)

½ cup chopped onion

½ cup Bisquick

3 eggs

1¼ cups milk

¼ teaspoon salt

⅛ teaspoon pepper

½ cup shredded cheddar or Swiss cheese

## DIRECTIONS

Preheat oven to 375°.

Cut bacon slices into thirds. Cook and stir bacon in a skillet over medium heat until almost crisp. Add onion. Cook, stirring frequently, until bacon is crisp. Drain. Spread bacon and onion in bottom of a lightly greased 1½-quart baking dish.

Beat Bisquick, eggs, milk, salt, and pepper in a large bowl using an electric mixer until almost smooth. Slowly pour egg mixture over bacon mixture; sprinkle cheese on top.

Bake, uncovered, about 35 minutes or until a knife inserted in center comes out clean.

Makes 4–6 servings.

# Impossible Quiche

## INGREDIENTS

12 slices bacon, diced (or 1 cup diced cooked ham)

⅓ cup finely chopped onion

1½ cups (6 ounces) shredded Swiss or cheddar cheese

1 (4-ounce) can sliced mushrooms, drained (optional)

6 tablespoons butter, melted

1½ cups milk

½ cup Bisquick

3 eggs

¼ teaspoon salt

⅛ teaspoon pepper

## DIRECTIONS

Preheat oven to 350°.

Cook bacon in a skillet over medium heat until crisp; remove from pan, reserving drippings, and crumble into a lightly greased deep, 10-inch pie plate. Sauté onion in drippings. Sprinkle onion, cheese, and mushrooms, if desired, evenly over bacon. In a blender, mix butter, milk, Bisquick, eggs, salt, and pepper on high speed for 1 minute (or use a hand mixer). Pour mixture into pie plate.

Bake 50–60 minutes or until golden brown and a knife inserted in the center comes out clean. Let stand for 5 minutes before cutting.

Makes 6–8 servings.

**Note:** You can prepare most of this before leaving for the cabin. Cook and crumble bacon, and sauté onion; place in separate zip-top plastic bags. Combine butter, milk, Bisquick, eggs, salt, and pepper in a quart jar. When you arrive at your cabin, just combine the ingredients, and this special supper is ready in 1 hour.

# Cottage Cheese Spinach Quiche

### INGREDIENTS

1 cup cottage cheese

1 (10-ounce) package frozen chopped spinach, thawed, well drained, and squeezed

3 eggs, beaten

1 scant teaspoon Lawry's seasoned salt

Sprinkle of nutmeg

½ cup Parmesan cheese

Butter

Paprika

### DIRECTIONS

Preheat oven to 350°.

Mix together cottage cheese, spinach, eggs, Lawry's, nutmeg, and Parmesan cheese. Pour mixture into a buttered 9-inch pie plate. Sprinkle with paprika.

Bake 30–45 minutes, until cooked through.

Makes 6 servings.

# Shrimp Pie

### INGREDIENTS

1 (8-ounce) can refrigerated crescent rolls

1½ cups shredded cheddar cheese, divided

3 eggs

1 (10.5-ounce) can cream of shrimp soup

¼ cup finely chopped celery

¼ cup finely chopped green bell pepper

2 tablespoons minced onion

Salt

Pepper

### DIRECTIONS

Preheat oven to 375°.

Spread out crescent roll dough in an ungreased 9x13-inch baking dish. Press on bottom and ½-inch up sides of dish to form crust. Sprinkle 1 cup cheese over dough. Beat eggs in a large bowl; mix in soup, celery, bell pepper, onion, salt, and pepper. Pour mixture over top. Sprinkle with remaining ½ cup cheese.

Bake, uncovered, 30–40 minutes or until a knife inserted in center comes out clean.

Makes 6–8 servings.

# Broccoli Soufflé

## INGREDIENTS

2 (10-ounce) packages frozen chopped broccoli or 2–3 heads fresh broccoli, chopped

½ cup chopped onion

4 tablespoons butter

2 tablespoons all-purpose flour

½ teaspoon salt

½ cup water

1 (8-ounce) jar Cheez Whiz

3 eggs, beaten

Cracker crumbs

## DIRECTIONS

Preheat oven to 325°.

Bring water to a boil over high heat in a large saucepan. Add broccoli; boil for 3–4 minutes. Drain and return to pan; cool slightly.

Sauté onions in butter in a skillet over medium heat. Add flour, salt, and ½ cup water, stirring until thick. Stir in Cheez Whiz.

Add eggs to broccoli; stir into cheese mixture. Pour into a lightly greased 1½-quart baking dish. Sprinkle with cracker crumbs.

Bake, uncovered, for 45 minutes.

Makes 6–8 servings.

# Gruyere Oven Omelet

## INGREDIENTS

8 eggs

1 cup milk

¼ pound Canadian bacon or ham, cut up

2½ cups (10 ounces) shredded Gruyere cheese

⅛ teaspoon nutmeg

Dash of salt

Dash of pepper

1 tablespoon melted butter

## DIRECTIONS

Preheat oven to 350°.

Beat eggs in a large bowl. Add milk, bacon, cheese, nutmeg, salt, and pepper. Pour into buttered 2-quart baking dish. Drizzle top with 1 tablespoon melted butter.

Bake, uncovered, for 40 minutes.

Makes 6–8 servings.

# Eggs Albuquerque

### INGREDIENTS

10 eggs

½ cup all-purpose flour

1 teaspoon baking powder

Dash of salt

½ cup butter, melted

1 (7-ounce) can diced green chiles, rinsed
and drained

2 cups cottage cheese

1 pound shredded Monterey Jack cheese

### DIRECTIONS

Preheat oven to 400°.

Beat eggs lightly in a large bowl. Stir in flour, baking
powder, and salt. Add butter, chiles, and cheeses.

Bake, uncovered, in 9x13-inch baking dish for
15 minutes. Reduce heat to 350°; bake additional
35–40 minutes. Cut into squares while warm.

Makes 6–8 servings.

 **Note:** This can be made ahead and stored
in the refrigerator until ready to bake.

# Ham 'n' Eggs

### INGREDIENTS

2 (4.2-ounce) boxes shredded hash browns

1½ cups diced ham

1½ cups shredded cheddar cheese

Green bell pepper, finely chopped (optional)

Onion, finely chopped (optional)

9 eggs, beaten

1½ cups milk

### DIRECTIONS

Soak hash browns in water until softened. Drain, and
pat into bottom of a 9x13-inch baking dish.

Preheat oven to 350°.

Layer ham and cheese over hash browns. Add bell
pepper and onion, if desired. Combine eggs and milk
in a large bowl. Pour over top.

Bake 45–60 minutes.

Makes 6 servings.

# Ham-and-Egg Pizza

## INGREDIENTS

1 (8-ounce) can refrigerated crescent rolls

¼ cup chopped onion

¼ cup butter

1 cup chopped ham (or cooked bacon or turkey)

4 eggs, beaten

½ cup milk

Dash of salt

Dash of pepper

1 cup shredded cheese (Swiss or Monterey Jack)

## DIRECTIONS

Preheat oven to 350°.

Press crescent rolls onto pizza pan to make crust. Sauté onion in butter in a skillet over medium heat; stir in ham. Spread mixture over crust.

Combine eggs, milk, salt, and pepper in a large bowl. Pour over ham and onion. Sprinkle cheese on top.

Bake 30 minutes or until brown.

Makes 3–4 servings.

Soups &
Sandwiches

# Overnight Barbecue Beef Sandwiches

*This is great for a crowd. Guests can help themselves when they are hungry.*

### INGREDIENTS

4–5 pounds boneless pork or beef roast

½ cup water

1 onion, sliced or chopped

1 (18-ounce) bottle barbecue sauce

Buns or French bread

### DIRECTIONS

Cook roast with ½ cup water in a slow cooker on low for 10 to 12 hours. Remove; cut into thin slices. Return to slow cooker. Add onion and barbecue sauce.

Cook on low 4–6 more hours. Serve on buns or French bread.

Makes 10–12 servings.

# Hot Ham and Cheese Sandwiches

### INGREDIENTS

½ cup (1 stick) butter, softened

2 tablespoons mustard

1 tablespoon poppy seeds

½ tablespoon Worcestershire sauce

2 tablespoons minced onion

6 sandwich rolls or rye buns

Sliced ham

6 slices Swiss cheese

### DIRECTIONS

Preheat oven to 350°.

Combine butter, mustard, poppy seeds, Worcestershire, and onion in a large bowl. Split rolls or buns. Spread butter mixture on top and bottom sides. Place ham and cheese on bottom sides, and replace tops. Wrap individually in aluminum foil.

Bake 15 minutes. Serve immediately.

Makes 6 servings.

**Note:** These sandwiches can be made in advance and refrigerated or frozen (and thawed) before baking. For appetizers, substitute 1 package of a dozen dinner rolls. Without separating rolls, slice in half horizontally. Spread with butter mixture. Place ham and cheese on bottom side, and replace top. Wrap in aluminum foil and bake 15–20 minutes; unwrap and cut into individual servings.

# Tuna-Cheese Melt

## INGREDIENTS

1 (5-ounce) can tuna, drained

2 tablespoons minced onion

2 tablespoons diced celery

1½ tablespoons mayonnaise

¼ teaspoon salt

¼ teaspoon pepper

2 English muffins, split

Butter

4 slices tomato

4 slices Swiss or American cheese

## DIRECTIONS

Preheat oven to 350°.

Combine tuna, onion, celery, mayonnaise, salt, and pepper in a small bowl. Toast and butter muffin halves. Divide tuna mixture evenly on muffin halves; top each with 1 tomato slice and 1 cheese slice. Place on a baking sheet.

Bake, uncovered, 5–7 minutes or until cheese is melted.

Makes 2 servings.

# Stovetop Hot Beef for Sandwiches

## INGREDIENTS

1 chuck roast

Vegetable oil

1 beef bouillon cube or 1 teaspoon instant beef bouillon granules per cup of water

1 package dry onion soup mix

1 cup tomato juice

Hamburger buns

## DIRECTIONS

Brown roast in oil over low heat in a large saucepan. Add water to cover. Add bouillon.

Simmer 3–5 hours or until most of the liquid is absorbed and meat can be easily shredded. Shred meat. Add soup mix and juice. Reheat. Serve on buns.

Makes 8–12 servings.

# Minnetonka Steak Sandwich

### DIP

½ cup butter

3 tablespoons Heinz 57 sauce

2 tablespoons sliced green onion

### SANDWICH

3 sirloin tip breakfast steaks, sliced very thin

French or sourdough bread

### DIRECTIONS

Combine butter, sauce, and green onion in a small saucepan over low heat. Cook until onion is soft.

In a hot skillet, fry steaks for about 3 minutes (1½ minutes on each side). Dip bread and steak into sauce before making 1 open-faced sandwich. Cut into 3 equal portions.


# Tuna-Filled Buns

### INGREDIENTS

1 cup diced or shredded cheddar cheese

3 hard-cooked eggs, diced

1 (5-ounce) can tuna, drained

2 tablespoons diced green bell pepper (optional)

2 tablespoons diced stuffed olives (optional)

2 tablespoons diced sweet pickles (optional)

½ cup mayonnaise

6 buns

### DIRECTIONS

Preheat oven to 250°.

Combine cheese and next 6 ingredients in a small bowl. Mix well. Divide evenly between 6 buns, and wrap each in aluminum foil. Place on a baking sheet.

Bake for 30 minutes.

Makes 6 servings.

**Note:** Make the filling at home, and transport it in an airtight container.

# Relaxed Roast Beef Sandwiches

## INGREDIENTS

1 (4-pound) rump roast or rolled chuck roast

Vegetable oil

3 beef bouillon cubes

2 cups boiling water

1 package dry onion soup mix

Buns

## DIRECTIONS

Preheat oven to 250°.

In an ovenproof pot, brown roast in oil on all sides. Dissolve bouillon in 2 cups boiling water; stir in soup mix. Pour over roast.

Cover roast, and bake about 3 hours, depending on desired doneness. Cool meat. Cut into thin slices, and return to juices in pot. (Be sure juices cover meat; add water, if necessary.) Let meat marinate in the refrigerator for 1 to 4 days.

When ready to use, heat slowly over low heat. Serve in buns as open-faced sandwiches, with juices on the side.

Makes 10–12 servings.

# Hot Dog Toasties

**INGREDIENTS**

8 hot dogs

8 slices of bread

Butter, softened

Mustard (optional)

8 slices American cheese

¼ cup butter, melted

**DIRECTIONS**

Drop hot dogs into boiling water over high heat. Reduce heat. Cover, and simmer 5–8 minutes.

Preheat broiler.

Spread bread slices with butter and, if desired, mustard. Place bread slices on a baking sheet or broiler pan. Top each bread slice with a slice of cheese. Place hot dogs diagonally on cheese. Fold bread over to form a triangle, and secure with toothpicks. Brush with ¼ cup melted butter.

Broil 3–4 inches from heat about 2 minutes or until toasted and golden brown.

Makes 8 servings.

# Open-Faced Cheeseburgers

**INGREDIENTS**

1 pound ground beef

1 teaspoon Worcestershire sauce

1 teaspoon oregano

½ teaspoon salt

Dash of pepper

1 cup shredded cheddar or American cheese

8 hamburger buns, split

**DIRECTIONS**

Preheat oven to 300°.

Mix together ground beef and next 5 ingredients. Spread mixture thinly on each hamburger bun half.

Bake 15–20 minutes. Watch carefully, and don't overcook.

# Baked Souper Sandwich

## INGREDIENTS

1½ pounds ground beef

1 small onion, chopped

½ cup chopped celery

½ teaspoon salt

4 cups herb-seasoned stuffing cubes

1½ cups milk

2 eggs, beaten

1 (10.5-ounce) can cream of mushroom soup

1 teaspoon dry mustard

1 cup shredded cheddar cheese

## DIRECTIONS

Preheat oven to 350°.

Brown beef, onion, and celery in a large skillet over medium heat. Drain, and stir in salt. Place stuffing cubes in a lightly greased 9x9-inch or 12x8-inch baking dish. Top with beef mixture. Combine milk, eggs, soup, and mustard in a bowl. Pour milk mixture over meat. Sprinkle with cheese.

Bake, uncovered, 30–40 minutes or until a knife inserted in center comes out clean. Cool for 5 minutes, and cut into squares.

Makes 6 servings.

# Sloppy Joes

## INGREDIENTS

1 pound ground beef

1 packet sloppy joe mix

1 (6-ounce) can tomato paste

1 (10.5-ounce) can chicken with rice soup

1 soup can of water

Hamburger buns

## DIRECTIONS

Brown ground beef in a large skillet over medium heat. Drain and return to skillet. Stir in sloppy joe mix, tomato paste, soup, and 1 soup can of water.

Reduce heat, and simmer for 30 minutes. Serve on toasted buns.

Makes 4 servings.

# Easiest Sloppy Joes

**INGREDIENTS**

1½ pounds ground beef

Chopped onion (optional)

1 (12-ounce) bottle Heinz chili sauce

Hamburger buns

**DIRECTIONS**

Brown ground beef and onion in a large skillet over medium heat. Drain and return to skillet. Add chili sauce and heat thoroughly. Serve on buns.

Makes 6 servings.


# Sloppy Josephs

**INGREDIENTS**

1 pound ground beef

½ cup chopped onion

1 (10.5-ounce) can chicken gumbo soup

3 tablespoons ketchup (or more, to taste)

1–2 tablespoons mustard

Hamburger buns

**DIRECTIONS**

Brown ground beef and onion in a large skillet over medium heat. Drain and return to skillet. Stir in soup, ketchup, and mustard; reduce heat, and simmer for 30 minutes. Serve on buns.

Makes 6 servings.

# Easy Pizzas

**INGREDIENTS**

1 package English muffins, split

1 jar pizza or marinara sauce

1 package sliced pepperoni

1 package shredded mozzarella cheese

**DIRECTIONS**

Preheat oven to 300°.

Place muffin halves on a baking sheet. Spread with sauce. Divide pepperoni evenly between muffins, covering sauce. Sprinkle cheese on top.

Bake 15–20 minutes, until cheese melts and begins to brown.

Makes 6–12 servings.

# Larry's Juicy Hamburgers

**INGREDIENTS**

2 pounds ground beef

½ cup grated apple

½ teaspoon salt

¼ teaspoon black pepper

¼ teaspoon Italian seasoning

2 eggs, beaten

½ cup cracker crumbs

10 hamburger buns

**DIRECTIONS**

Combine ground beef and next 6 ingredients. Form into 10 patties, and fry or broil until cooked through. Serve on buns.

Makes 10 servings.

**Note:** Patties can be made at home and frozen before taking to the cabin; allow to thaw in the refrigerator before cooking.

# Hearty Hamburger Soup

## INGREDIENTS

1½ pounds ground beef

1 small onion, chopped

4 carrots, peeled and chopped

2 stalks celery, chopped

2 (10.5-ounce) cans beef consommé

2 soup cans of water

½ cup barley

1 (28-ounce) can diced tomatoes

1 teaspoon salt

¼ teaspoon pepper

¼ teaspoon thyme

1 bay leaf

## DIRECTIONS

Brown ground beef and onion in a large soup pot over medium heat. Drain and return to pot. Add carrots and next 9 ingredients, and simmer for 1 hour. Remove bay leaf before serving.

Makes 8 servings.

 **Note:** This soup may be refrigerated for several days and also freezes well.

# Uncle Ole's Clam-Shrimp Chowder

## INGREDIENTS

12 slices bacon, diced

1 cup chopped onion

1 cup grated carrot

1 cup chopped celery

1 green bell pepper, finely chopped

4 cups milk

6 (10.5-ounce) cans potato soup

3 (10.75-ounce) cans tomato bisque soup

5 (6.5-ounce) cans minced clams, undrained

3 (4-ounce) cans small whole shrimp, drained

1 (2-ounce) jar diced pimientos

## SEASONINGS

Morton's seasoning blend, Lawry's seasoned salt, dried parsley, oregano, pepper

1 cup dry vermouth or wine (optional)

## DIRECTIONS

Cook bacon until crisp in a large skillet over medium heat. Remove bacon to a large bowl, leaving the bacon grease in the skillet. Sauté onion, carrot, celery, and bell pepper in bacon grease until tender. Drain vegetables and add to bowl with bacon.

In a large soup pot, combine milk, soups, clams and juice, shrimp, and pimientos. Bring to a simmer, stirring occasionally; add bacon and vegetables, and heat through. Stir in desired seasonings, to taste. Add vermouth, if desired.

Makes 12 servings.

# Navy Bean Soup

## INGREDIENTS

1 pound dry navy beans

1 teaspoon baking soda

1 ham hock with meat on it (or leftover ham, diced)

2 potatoes, peeled and diced

1 medium onion, diced

1½ teaspoons salt

Crackers or cornbread

## DIRECTIONS

Cover beans with water (1 inch above bean level) in a large soup pot. Add baking soda. Soak for at least 8 hours.

Drain beans and return to pot. Add ham hock, potatoes, onion, and salt. Barely cover all with water. Cover, and bring to a slow boil. Cook about 5 hours or until beans are tender. Remove bone. Serve with crackers or cornbread.

Makes 8 servings.

# Meatball Soup

## INGREDIENTS

1 pound ground beef

1 tablespoon minced onion

1 egg, beaten

½ cup breadcrumbs

¼ teaspoon salt

¼ teaspoon pepper

Vegetable oil

1 (14.5-ounce) can stewed tomatoes

1 (8-ounce) can tomato sauce

1 (15-ounce) can mixed vegetables

1 tablespoon sugar

1 cup water

1 envelope French onion soup mix

## DIRECTIONS

Combine ground beef, onion, egg, breadcrumbs, salt, and pepper in a large bowl. Shape mixture into small balls. Brown in oil in a large skillet over medium heat; drain. Place tomatoes and next 5 ingredients in a large soup pot, and bring to a boil.

Add meatballs, and simmer, covered, for 15 minutes.

Makes 6 servings.

# Salads & Dressings

# Pasta Vegetable Salad

## INGREDIENTS

1 (7-ounce) package macaroni rings

2 cups finely chopped cabbage

½ cup finely diced cucumber

½ cup finely diced green bell pepper

1 tablespoon finely diced onion

½ cup sugar

¼ cup vinegar

1 cup Miracle Whip

## DIRECTIONS

Prepare macaroni according to package directions. Drain and place in a large bowl. Stir in cabbage, cucumber, bell pepper, and onion. In a separate bowl, combine sugar, vinegar, and Miracle Whip. Pour over macaroni and vegetables, and mix well.

Makes 8 servings.

**Note:** Store salad in a 3-quart container in the refrigerator.

# Fresh Veggie Salad

*Make this a day ahead.*

## INGREDIENTS

- 1 head cauliflower, cut into bite-size pieces
- 1 bunch broccoli (2–3 heads), cut into bite-size pieces
- 1 large green bell pepper, chopped
- 1 sweet red onion, sliced into rings
- 1 container cherry tomatoes
- 1 (8-ounce) can sliced water chestnuts, drained
- 1 (6-ounce) can pitted ripe olives
- 2 envelopes Italian dressing and seasoning mix
- 1 tablespoon vegetable oil

## DIRECTIONS

Combine cauliflower and next 6 ingredients in a large bowl. In a separate bowl, mix salad dressing mix according to package instructions, adding an extra 1 tablespoon of oil. Add dressing to vegetables, and toss well. Cover and marinate overnight in the refrigerator.

Makes 12–14 servings.

 **Note:** Add ½ pound sliced fresh mushrooms and sliced celery.

# Tasty Marinated Vegetable Salad

*Make this a day ahead.*

## INGREDIENTS

1 (14.5-ounce) can green beans, drained

1 (14.5-ounce) can wax beans, drained

1 (14.5-ounce) can sliced carrots, drained

8 ounces whole button mushrooms, cleaned and halved or quartered

1 (2-ounce) jar diced pimientos, drained

1 onion, finely chopped

## MARINADE

½ cup vegetable oil

1½ cups sugar

1 cup vinegar

1 teaspoon salt

1 teaspoon celery seed

½ teaspoon paprika

Dash of garlic salt

## DIRECTIONS

Combine green beans and next 5 ingredients in a large bowl. To make marinade, whisk together oil and next 6 ingredients in a separate bowl; stir into vegetables.

Cover and let stand about 12 hours in the refrigerator, stirring occasionally.

Makes 10 servings.

 **Note:** After marinating for 12 hours, this salad may be frozen. It will also keep in the refrigerator for several days.

# Spinach Salad

## INGREDIENTS

1 pound fresh spinach, washed and drained

1 (14-ounce) can bean sprouts, well drained and squeezed

4 ounces fresh mushrooms, washed and sliced

1 onion, sliced and separated into rings

1 (8-ounce) can sliced water chestnuts, drained

8 ounces bacon, cooked and crumbled

## DRESSING

1 cup vegetable oil

¼ cup vinegar

½ cup sugar

1 tablespoon Worcestershire sauce

1 medium onion, grated

⅓ cup ketchup

½ teaspoon salt

## DIRECTIONS

Combine spinach, bean sprouts, mushrooms, onion, water chestnuts, and bacon in a large bowl.

To make dressing, combine oil and next 6 ingredients in a 1-quart jar. Shake well. Sprinkle over vegetables, and toss to coat.

Makes 6–8 servings.

# Overnight Layered Salad

*As the name implies, you make this the night before.*

## INGREDIENTS

1 head iceberg lettuce, washed, drained, and finely chopped

½ cup finely chopped green onion (tops included)

1 cup finely chopped celery (about 2 medium stalks)

½ (8-ounce) can sliced water chestnuts, drained

10 ounces uncooked frozen peas, thawed and drained

2 medium tomatoes, seeded and diced

### DRESSING

2 cups mayonnaise

1 teaspoon seasoned salt

¼ teaspoon garlic powder

### TOPPINGS

8 ounces bacon, cooked and crumbled

3 hard-cooked eggs, chopped

Parmesan cheese

## DIRECTIONS

Place lettuce in bottom of a 9x13-inch pan. Layer with green onion and next 4 ingredients.

To make dressing, combine mayonnaise, seasoned salt, and garlic powder in a large bowl; spread over top of salad.

Sprinkle with bacon, eggs, and cheese; refrigerate overnight.

Makes 10–12 servings.

# Summer Salad

## INGREDIENTS

10 radishes, sliced

2 cups chopped broccoli

3 cups chopped cauliflower

½ cup chopped celery

4–6 green onions (tops included), finely chopped

3–4 carrots, peeled and sliced into rounds

½ cup diced green bell pepper

Cherry tomatoes

Cucumbers, halved lengthwise, then sliced

## DRESSING

1 cup sour cream

½ cup mayonnaise

½ envelope garlic-and-herb salad dressing mix

## DIRECTIONS

Combine radishes and next 8 ingredients in a large bowl. To make dressing, combine sour cream, mayonnaise, and dressing mix in a separate bowl. Stir dressing into vegetables. Chill for 20 minutes before serving.

Makes 6–8 servings.

# Fresh Broccoli Salad

## INGREDIENTS

1 pound fresh broccoli, cut into bite-size pieces

2 tablespoons finely chopped green onions (tops included)

2 large tomatoes, seeded and chopped

½ cup mayonnaise

1 tablespoon lemon juice

½ teaspoon salt

¼ teaspoon pepper

## DIRECTIONS

Bring water to a boil in a large saucepan over high heat. Add broccoli and cook 1–2 minutes. Drain and rinse with cold water to stop the cooking process. Chill.

In a large bowl, combine broccoli, onions, and tomatoes.

To make dressing, combine mayonnaise, lemon juice, salt, and pepper in a small bowl; stir into vegetables.

Makes 4 servings.

# Marinated Carrots

**Make this at least a day ahead.**

## INGREDIENTS

2 pounds carrots, peeled and sliced

1 large onion, thinly sliced

1 large green bell pepper, cut into thin strips

1 (10.75-ounce) can tomato soup

1 cup sugar

½ cup vegetable oil

¾ cup vinegar

1 teaspoon salt

½ teaspoon pepper

¼ teaspoon dill weed

## DIRECTIONS

Cook carrots in water to cover in a saucepan over medium-high heat until just tender. Drain and cool. Put carrots, onion, and bell pepper in a large bowl. Add soup and next 6 ingredients to saucepan, and bring to a boil. Pour hot soup mixture over vegetables. Cover and let cool.

Refrigerate for at least 12 hours before serving.

Makes 8–10 servings.

 **Note:** This can be made at home and brought to the cabin. It will keep in the refrigerator for several days.

# Three-Bean Salad

*Make this the day before.*

## INGREDIENTS

1 (14.5-ounce) can green beans, drained

1 (14.5-ounce) can wax beans, drained

1 (16-ounce) can kidney beans, drained

1 small green bell pepper, diced

1 cup sliced celery

½ cup finely chopped onion

1 (4.5-ounce) jar whole mushrooms, drained

½ cup vegetable oil

¾ cup sugar

⅔ cup vinegar

½ teaspoon salt

½ teaspoon pepper

## DIRECTIONS

Combine green beans and next 6 ingredients in a large bowl. In a separate bowl, whisk together oil and next 4 ingredients, and stir into vegetables.

Marinate overnight before serving.

Makes 10–12 servings.

 **Note:** This travels well and keeps for days. For lunch, serve on a bed of shredded lettuce, with toast.

# Calypso Salad

## INGREDIENTS

1 (11-ounce) can Mexicorn, drained

4 cups shredded cabbage

¼ cup finely chopped onion

¼ cup cubed sharp cheddar cheese

¼ cup sliced black olives

## DRESSING

1 cup mayonnaise

2 tablespoons white vinegar

2 tablespoons sugar

1 tablespoon mustard

¼ teaspoon celery seed

Dash of salt

## DIRECTIONS

Combine Mexicorn and next 4 ingredients in a large bowl. To make dressing, whisk together mayonnaise and next 5 ingredients in a small bowl. Add to corn mixture, and mix well. Let stand 30 minutes before serving.

Makes 8–10 servings.

# Taco Salad

**INGREDIENTS**

1 pound ground beef

8 ounces shredded cheddar cheese

1 (16-ounce) can kidney beans, drained

1 or 2 tomatoes, chopped

Chopped onion

1 head iceberg lettuce, washed and torn up

1 (9.75-ounce) bag Doritos, crushed

2 avocadoes, chopped (optional)

Taco sauce

1 cup Thousand Island Dressing

**DIRECTIONS**

Brown ground beef in a large skillet over medium heat. Drain and place in a large bowl. Add cheese, beans, tomatoes, and onion; chill for a few hours. Just before serving, stir in lettuce, Doritos, and avocado. In a small bowl, mix together taco sauce and Thousand Island dressing. Toss with all ingredients.

Makes 4–6 servings.

# Middle Eastern Lentil Salad

**INGREDIENTS**

1 cup dried lentils

4 cups water

½ cup olive oil

5 tablespoons fresh lemon juice

3 tablespoons minced fresh parsley

2 cloves garlic, crushed

¾ teaspoon ground cumin

1 teaspoon salt

¼ teaspoon freshly ground pepper

Coriander (optional)

**DIRECTIONS**

Bring lentils and 4 cups water to a boil in a saucepan. Reduce heat. Simmer, uncovered, until lentils are firm-tender (about 30 minutes). While lentils are cooking, whisk together olive oil and next 6 ingredients in a medium bowl.

Drain lentils well; while still warm, add to olive oil mixture. Toss well. Arrange on a plate and serve. Sprinkle with coriander, if desired.

Makes 4–6 servings.

# Tuna Salad

## INGREDIENTS

2 (5-ounce) cans tuna, drained

3 green onions, finely chopped

3 stalks celery, finely chopped

½ cup mayonnaise

½ cup sour cream

2 tablespoons vinegar

2 tablespoons sugar

1 teaspoon salt

1 cup chow mein noodles

Lettuce

## DIRECTIONS

Combine tuna and next 7 ingredients. Just before serving, stir in noodles. Serve on lettuce.

Makes 4 servings.

# Make-Ahead Seafood Salad

*Make this the night before.*

## INGREDIENTS

¾ pound white bread slices

1 (6-ounce) can crabmeat, drained and flaked

2 (4-ounce) cans shrimp, drained

2 hard-cooked eggs, chopped

1½ cups mayonnaise

½ teaspoon salt

4 teaspoons lemon juice

¼ teaspoon dill weed

Dash of curry powder

Lettuce

## GARNISHES

Paprika, snipped fresh parsley

## DIRECTIONS

Trim crusts from bread and cut into ½-inch cubes. Combine bread cubes, crab, shrimp, and eggs in a large bowl. Combine mayonnaise and next 4 ingredients in a small bowl; stir into seafood mixture. Pat into a 9x9-inch baking dish.

Chill overnight. Cut into squares, and serve on lettuce. Garnish, if desired.

Makes 6–8 servings.

# Shrimp Salad

## INGREDIENTS

2 cups small shell pasta, cooked

1 green bell pepper, diced

1 medium-size onion, diced

2 (12-ounce) packages frozen cooked
small shrimp, thawed and drained

Sliced green olives (optional, to taste)

## DRESSING

3 egg yolks, well beaten

1¼ cups sugar

¾ cup vinegar

1 tablespoon all-purpose flour

1 tablespoon cornstarch

½ teaspoon salt

Dash of pepper

## DIRECTIONS

Combine pasta and next 4 ingredients in a large bowl.
To make dressing, cook egg yolks and next 6 ingredients
in a saucepan over medium heat until thick. Cool. Mix
dressing with pasta mixture. Cover and refrigerate.

Makes 6–8 servings.

# Easy Fruit Salad

### INGREDIENTS

1 (15.25-ounce) can pears or peaches, drained and cubed

1 (11-ounce) can mandarin oranges, drained

1 (8.25-ounce) can pineapple chunks, drained

1 (21-ounce) can peach or apricot pie filling

### DIRECTIONS

Combine all ingredients in a bowl. Refrigerate several hours before serving.

Makes 6–8 servings.

 **Note:** Try adding miniature marshmallows, sliced bananas, grapes, melon pieces, or other fresh fruit.


# Mandarin-Cashew Salad

### INGREDIENTS

2 heads iceberg lettuce, washed and torn into bite-size pieces

3 (11-ounce) cans mandarin oranges, drained

1 cup salted roasted cashews

1 medium-size onion, thinly sliced and divided into rings

Oil-and-vinegar salad dressing

### DIRECTIONS

Combine lettuce, oranges, cashews, and onion in a large bowl. Just before serving, toss with dressing.

Makes 10–12 servings.

# Blueberry Salad

## INGREDIENTS

1 (6-ounce) package strawberry gelatin mix

2 cups boiling water

1 (21-ounce) can blueberry pie filling

1 cup sour cream, at room temperature

## DIRECTIONS

Mix gelatin in 2 cups boiling water in a large bowl until it dissolves. Cool. Stir in blueberry pie filling and sour cream. Mix thoroughly. Chill until set.

Makes 8–10 servings.


# Simple Low-Calorie Salad

## INGREDIENTS

1 (0.6-ounce) box sugar-free lime gelatin mix

1½ cups boiling water

½ cup cold water

1 (20-ounce) can crushed pineapple in juice, undrained

1 (20-ounce) can pineapple chunks in juice, undrained

½–1 cup roasted nuts

Lettuce

Non-dairy whipped topping (optional)

## DIRECTIONS

Dissolve gelatin mix in 1½ cups boiling water in a large bowl. Add ½ cup cold water. Stir in crushed pineapple and pineapple chunks. Add nuts. Pour into a 9x9-inch glass baking dish.

Chill until firm. Cut into squares. Serve on lettuce. Top with whipped topping, if desired.

Makes 9 servings.

# Frozen Coleslaw

## INGREDIENTS

1 medium head cabbage, shredded

1 teaspoon salt

2 medium-size celery stalks, chopped

1 green bell pepper, chopped

2 carrots, grated

## DRESSING

1 cup vinegar

½ cup water

1½ cups sugar

1 teaspoon celery seed

1 teaspoon mustard seed

## DIRECTIONS

Mix cabbage with salt in a large bowl. Let stand for 1 hour. Drain liquid. Add celery, bell pepper, and carrots.

To make dressing, combine vinegar and next 4 ingredients in a saucepan. Bring to a boil, and boil for 1 minute. Cool. Pour over cabbage, and mix to combine. Freeze. Remove from freezer about 2 hours before serving.

Makes 6–8 servings.

 **Note:** Instead of freezing, this can be kept in the refrigerator for up to a week.

# Overnight Coleslaw

## INGREDIENTS

1 head cabbage, grated

2 carrots, grated

1 small green bell pepper, diced

1 (2-ounce) jar diced pimientos

1 small onion, finely grated

## DRESSING

1 cup sugar

1 cup vinegar

½ teaspoon salt

½ teaspoon celery seed

## DIRECTIONS

Mix cabbage and next 4 ingredients in a large bowl.

To make dressing, combine sugar and next 3 ingredients in a saucepan. Bring to a boil. While hot, pour over vegetables. Let stand overnight.

Makes 6–8 servings.

# Cabin German Potato Salad

## INGREDIENTS

1 chopped onion

6 bacon strips, cut into pieces

2 (15-ounce) cans German potato salad

2 tablespoons brown sugar

## DIRECTIONS

Sauté onion and bacon pieces in a large skillet over medium heat. Drain fat from pan. Stir in potato salad. Heat thoroughly. Sprinkle brown sugar on top. Heat 5 more minutes before serving.

Makes 5–6 servings.

# Old-Fashioned Potato Salad

## INGREDIENTS

2½–3 cups peeled and cubed cooked potatoes

1 teaspoon vinegar

1 teaspoon sugar

½ cup sliced celery

2 hard-cooked eggs, chopped

⅓ cup finely chopped onion

1 teaspoon salt

¾ teaspoon celery seed

¾ cup mayonnaise

## GARNISHES

Fresh parsley sprig, 1 sliced hard-cooked egg

## DIRECTIONS

Place warm potato cubes in a large bowl; sprinkle with vinegar and sugar. Toss with a fork. Set aside for about 1 hour.

Add celery and chopped eggs to potatoes. In a separate bowl, mix onion, salt, celery seed, and mayonnaise in a small bowl. Add to potato and egg mixture, and toss to coat. Refrigerate until thoroughly chilled.

Makes 6 servings.

Main
Dishes

# Calico Bean Casserole

## INGREDIENTS

½ pound bacon, diced

2 pounds ground beef

1 cup chopped onion

1 cup chopped celery

1 (15-ounce) can pork and beans in tomato sauce

1 (16-ounce) can kidney beans, drained

1 (15.25-ounce) can lima beans, drained

1 (16-ounce) can butter beans, drained

1 cup ketchup

3 tablespoons vinegar

1 teaspoon dry mustard

½ cup brown sugar

1 teaspoon salt

## DIRECTIONS

Preheat oven to 350°.

Cook bacon in a large skillet over medium heat; drain and remove to a large bowl. Brown beef in skillet, adding onions and celery toward the end; drain.

Combine pork and beans and next 8 ingredients with bacon in large bowl. Add beef mixture and stir to combine. Pour into a baking dish.

Bake, covered, for 45 minutes.

Makes 10–12 servings.

**Note:** This can be cooked in a slow cooker on low heat for 6 to 8 hours. It keeps in the refrigerator for several days and freezes well.

# Corn Sausage Casserole

### INGREDIENTS

1 pound bulk pork sausage

4 eggs, beaten

2½ cups cream-style corn

1 cup breadcrumbs

1 teaspoon salt

⅛ teaspoon pepper

¼–½ cup ketchup

### DIRECTIONS

Preheat oven to 350°.

Brown sausage in a large skillet over medium heat. Drain. Combine eggs and next 4 ingredients in large bowl; stir in sausage. Pour into a greased 10x6-inch baking dish.

Bake, uncovered, for 30 minutes. Spread ketchup on top. Bake for 10 more minutes.

Makes 6 servings.


# Dried Beef Casserole

**Allow at least 4 hours for this recipe.**

### INGREDIENTS

1 (10.5-ounce) can cream of mushroom soup

1 cup milk

1 cup shredded cheddar cheese

3 tablespoons finely chopped onion

1 cup elbow macaroni, cooked according to package directions

½ pound dried beef, soaked in boiling water, drained, and roughly chopped

2 hard-cooked eggs, diced

### DIRECTIONS

In a large bowl, stir together soup and milk to a creamy consistency. Stir in cheese and next 3 ingredients. Gently fold in eggs. Transfer to a buttered 2-quart baking dish. Refrigerate at least 3 hours or overnight.

Preheat oven to 350°.

Bake, uncovered, for 1 hour.

Makes 4 servings.

# Easy Chili

## INGREDIENTS

1 pound ground beef

1 onion, chopped

¾ teaspoon salt

¼ teaspoon pepper

1 cup chopped celery

2 (15-ounce) cans kidney beans or
   chili beans, drained

1 (46-ounce) can tomato juice

1 tablespoon chili powder
   (more or less, to taste)

## DIRECTIONS

Brown beef and onion in a Dutch oven or large pot over medium heat. Drain grease from beef mixture. Add salt and pepper, then stir in celery, beans, tomato juice, and chili powder. Simmer for at least 1 hour.

Makes 4–6 servings.

# Chicken-Vegetable-French Fry Casserole

## INGREDIENTS

1 (3–4 pound) package cut-up bone-in chicken or 2 pounds boneless skinless chicken breasts

¾ cup butter (1½ sticks), divided

¼ cup all-purpose flour

1 teaspoon salt

1 (10.5-ounce) can cream of celery soup

1 (12-ounce) package frozen peas and carrots

16 ounces frozen French fries

Parmesan cheese

## DIRECTIONS

Place chicken in a large soup pot with enough water to cover, and simmer for an hour, skimming any foam that accumulates on the surface. Remove chicken pieces to cool, reserving 2 cups stock. (Save any remaining stock for future use.) Debone chicken, trim fat, and cut into pieces. Spread chicken in bottom of a buttered 9x13-inch baking dish.

Preheat oven to 450°.

In a medium saucepan, melt ¼ cup butter; whisk flour into butter, and then add salt, reserved 2 cups stock, and soup. Cook, stirring occasionally, until thick and smooth; remove from heat. Cook peas and carrots for 3 minutes, and drain. Mix into sauce, then pour over chicken.

Melt ½ cup butter in a large skillet, and stir frozen French fries in it until coated. Place fries on top of other ingredients. Sprinkle generously with Parmesan cheese.

Bake, uncovered, 20–25 minutes.

Makes 8 servings.

 **Note:** Cook the chicken at home before leaving for the cabin.

# Hamburger–Wild Rice Casserole

## INGREDIENTS

1 cup wild rice, rinsed

4 cups boiling water

¼ cup finely chopped onion

1½ pounds ground beef

1 (10.5-ounce) can cream of mushroom soup

1 (10.5-ounce) can cream of chicken soup

1 (4-ounce) can sliced mushrooms, drained

1 (8-ounce) can sliced water chestnuts, drained

2 beef bouillon cubes in 1 cup boiling water

½ teaspoon salt (or celery salt)

¼ teaspoon pepper

## DIRECTIONS

Preheat oven to 350°.

Put rice in a soup pot, and cover with 4 cups boiling water. Simmer for 5 minutes. Remove from heat, and let stand 15 minutes before draining; return rice to pot. Brown onion and ground beef in a large skillet over medium heat. Drain. Add beef mixture, soups, and next 5 ingredients to pot; stir to combine. Transfer to a large baking dish.

Bake for 1½ hours, covering for first 45 minutes.

Makes 8–10 servings.

# Easy Stove-Top Stew for 4

## INGREDIENTS

1 pound stew meat

1 tablespoon vegetable oil

1 teaspoon salt

1 (10.75-ounce) can tomato soup

1 soup can of water

3 carrots, peeled and chopped

3 potatoes, chopped

3 small onions, chopped

## DIRECTIONS

Brown meat in oil in a large skillet over medium heat. Add salt. Stir in soup and 1 can water.

Cover and simmer 1½ hours. Add carrots, potatoes, and onion. Return to a simmer, and cook for 30 minutes. (If it starts to become dry, add a little more water.)

Makes 4 servings.

# Can Opener Casserole

## INGREDIENTS

1 (10.5-ounce) can cream of mushroom soup

1 (10.5-ounce) can cream of chicken soup

1 (12-ounce) can evaporated milk

2 (10-ounce) cans chunk chicken, drained

1 (4-ounce) can sliced mushrooms, drained

1 cup chopped celery (sautéed in butter)

2 cups chow mein noodles

## GARNISHES

Slivered almonds and jarred diced
   pimientos, drained

## DIRECTIONS

Preheat oven to 350°.

Combine soups and next 5 ingredients in a large bowl; transfer to a 2-quart baking dish.

Bake, covered, for 1 hour. Garnish, if desired.

Makes 6–8 servings.

# Cabin Stew

## INGREDIENTS

2 pounds cubed stew meat

1 (14.5-ounce) can diced tomatoes

1 (12-ounce) bag frozen peas

6 carrots, peeled and sliced

1 large onion, chopped

1 cup celery, chopped

3 medium-size potatoes, diced

2 tablespoons sugar

1 tablespoon salt

¼ teaspoon pepper

¼ cup quick tapioca

¼ cup dry red wine

1 (8-ounce) can sliced water chestnuts, drained (optional)

## DIRECTIONS

Preheat oven to 275°.

Combine meat, next 11 ingredients, and, if desired, water chestnuts in a large bowl. Transfer to a large baking dish.

Cover and bake for at least 5 hours.

Makes 8 servings.

 **Note:** No need to brown the meat with this recipe.

# Hunters' Stew

## INGREDIENTS

4 slices bacon, cut into 1-inch pieces

1 tablespoon butter or vegetable oil

1 pound cubed stew meat

2 large onions (about 2 cups), chopped

3 medium-size apples (about 2 cups), peeled, quartered, cored, and chopped

1 (10.5-ounce) can beef consommé

2 cups water

1½ teaspoons salt

2 cups carrots, peeled and diced

1 pound Polish sausage, cut into 1½-inch lengths

1 small head cabbage, shredded (about 4 cups)

## DIRECTIONS

Cook bacon in a heavy soup pot or Dutch oven until crisp. Remove to drain on paper towels, reserving drippings in pot, and set aside. Add butter to drippings in kettle. Brown beef (in batches, if necessary), turning to brown well on all sides. Stir in onion and apple, and cook about 5 minutes or until apple is tender. Add consommé, 2 cups water, and salt. Cover.

Simmer 1 hour and 20 minutes. Add carrots and sausage, and simmer 30 minutes more. Add cabbage and reserved bacon. Simmer 10 minutes or until cabbage is tender.

Makes 8 servings.

**Note:** The stew may also be cooked in a slow cooker for 6 hours on high (8 hours on low). Place all ingredients in a slow cooker at the same time. You can also omit the cabbage, substitute 1½ pounds ground beef for stew meat, and reduce the amount of Polish sausage to ½ pound.

# Old-Time Beef Stew

## INGREDIENTS

2 pounds beef chuck, cut into bite-size pieces

2 tablespoons vegetable oil

4 cups boiling water

1 tablespoon lemon juice

1 teaspoon Worcestershire sauce

1 whole garlic clove, peeled (on toothpick for easy removal)

1 medium onion, sliced

1–2 bay leaves

1 tablespoon salt

1 teaspoon sugar

½ teaspoon pepper

4 large carrots, sliced

4 large potatoes, diced

¼ cup all-purpose flour

½ cup cold water

## DIRECTIONS

Brown meat in oil in a large soup pot over medium heat. Add 4 cups boiling water, lemon juice, and next 7 ingredients. Cover. Simmer for 2 hours, stirring occasionally. Remove bay leaves and garlic. Add carrots and potatoes.

Cover and cook 30 minutes or until vegetables are done. Remove meat and vegetables to a bowl, reserving broth in pot; keep warm. Skim excess fat from broth. In a small bowl, mix flour into ½ cup cold water, then slowly add to broth, whisking to incorporate. Cook for 5 minutes or until thickened to make gravy. Add meat and vegetables back to the pot to combine.

Makes 8 servings.

# Chow Mein

## INGREDIENTS

2 pounds diced pork or beef

1 teaspoon pepper

1½ cups (or more) chopped celery

1 large onion, chopped

1 (14-ounce) can bean sprouts, drained (reserve liquid)

1 (8-ounce) can sliced water chestnuts

Fresh mushrooms, cleaned and sliced

1 beef bouillon cube in ½ cup boiling water

1 (10.5-ounce) can cream of mushroom soup

1 (6-ounce) can mushroom steak sauce

1 tablespoon molasses

3 tablespoons soy sauce

2 tablespoons cornstarch

Hot cooked rice or chow mein noodles

## DIRECTIONS

Brown meat in a large soup pot over medium heat; add pepper. Stir in celery and next 9 ingredients.

Simmer, covered, 1¼ hours. In a small bowl, mix cornstarch with enough of the bean sprout liquid to make a slurry, and stir into the chow mein to thicken. Serve over rice or chow mein noodles.

Makes 8 servings.

# Chow Mein Hot Dish

## INGREDIENTS

1 pound ground beef

2 cups diced celery

1 large onion, chopped

1 cup uncooked rice

2½ cups hot water

1 (10.5-ounce) can cream of mushroom soup

4 tablespoons soy sauce

1 tablespoon brown sugar

1½ cups salted cocktail peanuts

## DIRECTIONS

Preheat oven to 400°.

Cook beef, celery, and onion in a large skillet over medium heat. Drain mixture and return to skillet. Add rice and next 4 ingredients, and mix well. Transfer to a large baking dish.

Bake, uncovered, for 45 minutes. Sprinkle peanuts over top. Bake 15 more minutes.

Makes 6 servings.

# Ground Beef Stir-Fry

**INGREDIENTS**

1½ pounds ground beef

2 tablespoons vegetable oil

¼ cup soy sauce

1 green bell pepper, cut up

3 carrots, peeled and thinly sliced

2 onions, sliced and cut into half rings

4 stalks celery, sliced diagonally

Fresh or canned mushrooms

1 tablespoon cornstarch

½ cup beef consommé (freeze the rest for later use)

Hot cooked rice

**DIRECTIONS**

Brown ground beef in oil in a large skillet or wok; drain and return to skillet. Add soy sauce and next 5 ingredients. Cover and cook 5 minutes or until crisp-tender, stirring occasionally.

In a small bowl, dissolve cornstarch in consommé. Add to meat and vegetables to thicken. Serve over rice.

Makes 6 servings.

# Cheeseburger Pie

## INGREDIENTS

1 pound ground beef

1½ cups chopped onion

½ teaspoon salt

¼ teaspoon pepper

1 cup (4 ounces) shredded cheddar cheese

1½ cups milk

¾ cup Bisquick

3 eggs

Shredded iceberg lettuce (optional)

Sliced fresh tomato (optional)

## DIRECTIONS

Preheat oven to 400°.

Brown ground beef with onion in a large skillet over medium heat. Drain and return to skillet. Stir in salt and pepper. Spread in bottom of a lightly greased 10-inch pie plate. Sprinkle with cheese.

Beat milk, Bisquick, and eggs in a blender for 15 seconds on high speed (or whisk by hand for 1 minute) or until smooth. Pour over cheese.

Bake about 30 minutes or until golden brown. Let stand 5 minutes before cutting. Top individual servings with cold shredded lettuce and tomato slices, if desired. Refrigerate any remaining pie.

Makes 6 servings.

 **Note:** If using a 9-inch pie plate, decrease milk to 1 cup, Bisquick to ½ cup, and eggs to 2.

# Spaghetti Pie

## INGREDIENTS

6 ounces dry spaghetti

2 tablespoons butter

½ cup grated Parmesan cheese

2 eggs, well beaten

1 cup cottage cheese

1 pound ground beef

½ cup finely chopped green onion (tops included)

¼ cup chopped green bell pepper

½ cup chopped tomatoes (fresh or canned)

1 (6-ounce) can tomato paste

1 teaspoon sugar

1 teaspoon oregano

½ teaspoon garlic salt

½ cup shredded mozzarella cheese

## DIRECTIONS

Preheat oven to 350°.

Cook spaghetti according to package directions for al dente, and drain. In a large bowl, stir butter into spaghetti. Add Parmesan and eggs, and mix well. Press noodle mixture into bottom of a buttered 10-inch pie plate. Spread cottage cheese over spaghetti crust.

Brown beef with onion and bell pepper in a large skillet over medium heat. Drain and return to skillet. Stir in tomatoes, tomato paste, sugar, oregano, and garlic salt. Spread meat mixture over cottage cheese. Top with mozzarella cheese.

Bake, uncovered, for 30 minutes (longer, if frozen) or until bubbly. Recipe can easily be doubled to make 2 pies.

Makes 6 servings.

 **Note:** Prepare ahead of time, and refrigerate or freeze until ready to bake.

# Make-Ahead Spaghetti Sauce or Chili Base

## INGREDIENTS

4 pounds ground beef

2 cups chopped onions

1 cup chopped green bell pepper

2 cups chopped celery

1 (15-ounce) can tomato sauce

1 (12-ounce) can tomato paste

4 cups chopped tomatoes (fresh or canned)

2 tablespoons sugar

2 teaspoons salt

2 whole garlic cloves, peeled (on toothpicks, for easy removal)

2 bay leaves

½ teaspoon oregano

## DIRECTIONS

Brown beef in a large skillet (in batches, if necessary). Midway through the browning, add onions, bell pepper, and celery. Drain and return to skillet. Add tomato sauce and next 7 ingredients. Simmer for 2 hours. Remove garlic and bay leaves.

Makes 16 servings.

**Note:** Freeze this sauce in meal-size containers to use as needed. To make into chili, add chili powder and canned chili beans or kidney beans (drained) to taste.

# Meatballs

## INGREDIENTS

1 bouillon cube

½ cup hot water

¾ cup milk, divided

1 cup soft breadcrumbs

2 pounds ground beef

½ cup minced onion

1 teaspoon sugar

1 teaspoon seasoned salt

1 egg

1 (10.5-ounce) can cream of
mushroom soup

## DIRECTIONS

Preheat oven to 350°.

In a large bowl, dissolve bouillon cube in ½ cup hot water. Add ½ cup milk and next 6 ingredients, and mix well. Shape into small meatballs. Place on a baking sheet.

Bake, uncovered, for 30 minutes. Place meatballs in a baking dish. In a small bowl, stir together soup and remaining ¼ cup milk. Spread on top. Bake 30 more minutes.

Makes 6–8 servings.

**Note:** These freeze well.

# One-Pan Spaghetti

## INGREDIENTS

1 pound ground beef

½ cup chopped onion

1 (14.5-ounce) can whole tomatoes

2 cups tomato juice

1 (8-ounce) can tomato sauce

1½ teaspoons sugar

1½ teaspoons oregano

¾ teaspoon garlic powder

1 teaspoon Worcestershire sauce

½ teaspoon salt

½ (7-ounce) package spaghetti, uncooked and broken

Parmesan cheese

## DIRECTIONS

Brown beef and onion in a large skillet over medium heat. Drain and return to skillet. Add tomatoes and next 7 ingredients. Bring mixture to a boil. Mix in spaghetti.

To cook on the stovetop: Cover tightly, and simmer for 40 minutes, stirring occasionally. Uncover, and simmer for an additional 15 minutes.

To cook in the oven: Bake at 325°, covered, for 1 hour, stirring occasionally. Uncover, and bake for another 30 minutes.

Sprinkle Parmesan cheese on top just before serving.

Makes 4 servings.

# Meat and Macaroni Dinner

## INGREDIENTS

1 pound ground beef

¼ cup chopped onion

1 cup elbow macaroni, cooked and drained

1 (10.5-ounce) can cheddar cheese soup

⅓ cup water

¼ teaspoon pepper

## DIRECTIONS

Brown beef and onion in a large skillet over medium heat. Drain and return to skillet. Stir in macaroni and next 3 ingredients. Heat thoroughly, and serve.

Makes 4 servings.

# Do-Ahead Lasagna

## INGREDIENTS

1 pound ground beef

1 tablespoon dried chopped onion

2 teaspoons salt

1 tablespoon sugar

1 teaspoon chili powder

1 teaspoon garlic salt

1½ teaspoons basil or oregano

1 (12-ounce) can tomato paste

1 (15-ounce) can tomato sauce

3½ cups water

3 cups shredded mozzarella cheese

12 lasagna noodles, uncooked

## DIRECTIONS

Preheat oven to 350°.

Brown beef in a large skillet over medium heat. Drain and return to skillet. Stir in onion, salt, sugar, chili powder, garlic salt, and basil. Add tomato paste, tomato sauce, and 3½ cups water. Bring to a boil; simmer 10 minutes. (Mixture will be thin.)

Spoon about 1½ cups sauce into bottom of a 9x13-inch baking dish. Cover the sauce with 4 uncooked noodles. Spoon more sauce to cover noodles. Sprinkle ⅓ of cheese over sauce. Repeat layers two more times. Cover with aluminum foil.

Bake for 1 hour. Uncover and bake 30 more minutes.

Makes 6 servings.

**Note:** Lasagna may be made ahead and stored in the refrigerator. Increase covered baking time by 30 minutes.

# Pot Roast Meat Loaf

## INGREDIENTS

1 pound lean ground beef

⅔ cup evaporated milk

⅓ cup fine breadcrumbs

¼ cup ketchup

1 teaspoon salt

2 teaspoons Worcestershire sauce

Dash of pepper

3 medium potatoes, peeled and sliced

3 medium onions, sliced

3 medium carrots, peeled and sliced

2 teaspoons dried parsley flakes

1 teaspoon salt

## DIRECTIONS

Preheat oven to 375°.

Combine beef and next 6 ingredients. Shape into a loaf, and place in a 9x13-inch baking dish. Place potatoes, onion, and carrots in layers around meat. Sprinkle with parsley flakes and salt. Cover with aluminum foil.

Bake for 1 hour or until vegetables are tender. Remove foil, and bake 10 more minutes.

Makes 4 servings.

# Good Neighbor's Hot Dish with Sour Cream

## INGREDIENTS

1½ pounds ground beef

1 cup chopped onion

3 cups uncooked medium-size noodles
(macaroni, shells, rotini, etc.)

3 cups tomato juice

1 teaspoon salt

1½ teaspoons celery salt

Dash of pepper

2 teaspoons Worcestershire sauce

¼ green bell pepper, chopped

1 (4-ounce) can sliced mushrooms,
drained (optional)

1 cup sour cream

## DIRECTIONS

Brown beef and onion in a large skillet over medium heat. Drain and return mixture to skillet. Add noodles, next 6 ingredients, and, if desired, mushrooms. Cook until noodles are tender. Add sour cream, and gently heat through (don't boil).

Makes 6–8 servings.

# Knobby Pines Goulash

## INGREDIENTS

1½ pounds ground beef

1½ cups chopped celery

2 onions, chopped

2 beef bouillon cubes

½ cup hot water

1 (10.75-ounce) can tomato soup

1 (14.5-ounce) can stewed tomatoes

½ (16-ounce) package egg noodles, cooked and drained

1 teaspoon salt

1 (8-ounce) can sliced water chestnuts, drained (optional)

## DIRECTIONS

Preheat oven to 350°.

Brown beef, celery, and onion in a large skillet over medium heat. Drain and return mixture to skillet. In a small bowl, dissolve bouillon cubes in ½ cup hot water; add to skillet. Stir in soup and next 3 ingredients. Transfer to a 2-quart baking dish.

Cover and bake for 30 minutes. Add water chestnuts, if desired; cover, and bake 30 more minutes.

Makes 8 servings.

# Swedish Meatballs

**INGREDIENTS**

1 pound ground beef

½ cup fine breadcrumbs

1 egg

⅔ cup milk

¼ cup minced onion

½ teaspoon salt

⅛ teaspoon pepper

¼ teaspoon nutmeg

1 (10.5-ounce) can cream of mushroom soup

¼ cup water

**DIRECTIONS**

Preheat oven to 325°.

Combine beef and next 7 ingredients. Form into small balls.

Brown slowly in a large skillet; drain. Place in a 1-quart baking dish. In a small bowl, dilute soup with ¼ cup water. Pour mixture over meatballs.

Bake for 1 hour.

Makes 4 servings.

# Taco Pie

**INGREDIENTS**

1 pound ground beef

1 (8-ounce) can tomato sauce

½ cup water

1 envelope taco seasoning

1 (8-ounce) can refrigerated crescent rolls

2 cups crushed tortilla chips, divided

1 cup sour cream

1 cup shredded mozzarella cheese

**DIRECTIONS**

Preheat oven to 375°.

Brown beef in a large skillet over medium heat. Drain and return to skillet. Add tomato sauce, ½ cup water, and taco seasoning. Simmer for 5 minutes.

Unroll and press crescent roll dough in bottom of 10-inch pie plate, pinching pieces together to make a crust. Layer, in order, 1 cup crushed chips, beef mixture, sour cream, cheese, and remaining 1 cup crushed chips

Bake for 25 minutes.

Makes 6 servings.

# Aunt Linnea's Five-Decker Dinner

## INGREDIENTS

6 slices of bacon, cut into 1-inch pieces

1 pound ground beef, shaped into 4 patties

1 teaspoon salt

½ teaspoon pepper

4 onions, sliced

4 medium potatoes, sliced

4–6 carrots, peeled and sliced

¼ cup chopped green bell pepper

1 tablespoon chopped parsley (optional)

¼ cup water

## DIRECTIONS

Place bacon pieces on the bottom of an electric skillet or Dutch oven. Put ground beef patties on the bacon. Sprinkle with salt and pepper. Layer onions, potatoes, and carrots on top, adding more salt and pepper. Put bell pepper and parsley, if desired, on top.

Cook on medium heat until bacon is sizzling, 3–5 minutes. Add ¼ cup water. Cover, and turn heat to low. Cook about 45 minutes. Drain grease.

Makes 4 servings.

# Texas Straw Hats

## INGREDIENTS

1 cup chopped onion

⅔ cup chopped celery

⅔ cup chopped green bell pepper

3 tablespoons vegetable oil

2 pounds ground beef

2–3 teaspoons chili powder

2 teaspoons salt

¼ teaspoon pepper

2 (6-ounce) cans tomato paste

½ cup ketchup

2 cups water

2 teaspoons Worcestershire sauce

Dash of Tabasco sauce

2 (9.25-ounce) packages corn chips

Shredded American or sharp
    cheddar cheese

## DIRECTIONS

In a large skillet over medium heat, cook onion, celery, and bell pepper in oil until tender. Remove from pan and set aside. Brown beef in skillet; drain and return to skillet. Stir in onion, celery, and bell pepper. Add chili powder and next 7 ingredients.

Simmer, uncovered, for 1 hour, stirring occasionally. Serve over corn chips. Top generously with cheese.

Makes 8 servings.

 **Note:** This keeps in the refrigerator for several days.

# Lake Dogs with Beans

### INGREDIENTS

½ cup butter, softened

2 tablespoons mustard

2 tablespoons Parmesan cheese

1 tablespoon finely chopped green bell pepper

1 tablespoon chopped onion

8 hot dog buns

8 hot dogs

1 (15-ounce) can pork and beans

### DIRECTIONS

Cream butter in a large bowl. Add mustard, cheese, bell pepper, and onion; mix well. Open each bun and place on a double-thick rectangle of aluminum foil. Spread butter mixture on both sides of split buns. Slit hot dogs lengthwise, cutting to but not through the other side. Place each split hot dog in a bun, and fill each cavity with beans. Fold foil over each sandwich.

Grill for 10 minutes on each side, or bake at 350° for 15 minutes.

Makes 8 servings.

# Cabin Supper Special

### INGREDIENTS

8 hot dogs

¼ cup Cheez Whiz (or other cheese)

Milk

1–2 tablespoons minced onion

2 cups mashed potatoes (instant is fine)

Paprika

### DIRECTIONS

Preheat broiler.

Cook hot dogs; cool slightly. Over medium-low heat, melt cheese in a medium-size saucepan, adding a small amount of milk to thin and stirring often, being careful not to burn. Stir in minced onion. Add potatoes, and heat through, stirring often.

Split hot dogs lengthwise, and spoon potato mixture on top. Sprinkle with paprika.

Broil until lightly browned.

Makes 4 servings.

# Ham Au Gratin

## INGREDIENTS

¼ cup vegetable oil

1 pound frozen hash browns

Butter

1 pound ham, cut into bite-size pieces

1 cup plain yogurt, at room temperature

1 (10.5-ounce) can cheddar cheese soup

½ teaspoon mustard

## DIRECTIONS

Preheat oven to 400°.

Heat oil and brown hash browns in a large skillet over medium heat. Cover and cook 4 minutes; uncover and cook 8 minutes or until golden, turning once. Put hash browns in a buttered 9-inch-square baking dish. Cover with ham cubes. Combine yogurt, soup, and mustard in a small bowl. Pour over top.

Bake  20–25 minutes.

Makes 4–6 servings.

# Chicken and Broccoli, Minnesota Style

## INGREDIENTS

1 (3–4 pound) package cut-up bone-in chicken or 2 pounds boneless skinless chicken breasts

2 pounds frozen broccoli

1 (10.5-ounce) can cream of mushroom soup

2 (10.5-ounce) cans cream of chicken soup

1¼ soup cans of water

1 (4-ounce) can sliced mushrooms, undrained

Parmesan cheese

## DIRECTIONS

Preheat oven to 325°.

In a covered soup pot, simmer chicken in a small amount of water until tender, about an hour. Remove skin and bones. Cut chicken into small pieces. Cook broccoli in water to cover in a saucepan over medium-high heat until crisp-tender. Alternate layers of chicken and broccoli in a 9x13-inch baking dish.

In a large bowl, mix soups with 1¼ soup cans of water. Stir in mushrooms and liquid. Pour over chicken and broccoli. Sprinkle with Parmesan cheese.

Bake 45–60 minutes.

Makes 8 servings.

# Zucchini Crescent Pie

## INGREDIENTS

4 cups thinly sliced, unpeeled zucchini

1 cup coarsely chopped onion

½ cup butter

½ cup chopped fresh parsley or
  2 tablespoons parsley flakes

½ teaspoon salt

¼ teaspoon black pepper

¼ teaspoon garlic powder (or salt)

¼ teaspoon sweet basil leaves

¼ teaspoon oregano leaves

2 eggs, well beaten

8 ounces (2 cups) shredded
  mozzarella cheese

1 (8-ounce) can refrigerated
  crescent rolls

2 teaspoons prepared
  Dijon mustard

## DIRECTIONS

Preheat oven to 350°.

In a 10-inch skillet, cook zucchini and onion in butter until tender—about 10 minutes. In a large bowl, combine parsley and next 5 ingredients. Blend in eggs and cheese. Stir in zucchini mixture.

Separate dough into 8 triangles. Press into an ungreased 10-inch pie plate. Press on bottom and up sides, pinching pieces together to form a crust. Spread mustard onto crust. Pour zucchini mixture evenly into crust.

Bake 18–20 minutes.

Makes 6 servings.

# Chicken and Stuffing Hot Dish

## INGREDIENTS

1 (6-ounce) box stuffing mix for chicken

1 (9-ounce) package frozen broccoli spears

3 boneless skinless chicken breasts

1 (10.5-ounce) can cream of chicken soup

1 soup can of water

1 cup shredded Colby cheese

## DIRECTIONS

Preheat oven to 350°.

Prepare stuffing mix according to package directions. Place in bottom of a lightly greased 8x11-inch baking dish. Cook broccoli in water to cover in a saucepan over medium-high heat until crisp-tender. Place on top of stuffing. Cook chicken breasts in a skillet over medium heat; cut into bite-size pieces and layer over broccoli. Mix soup with 1 soup can of water. Spread over top, and sprinkle with cheese. Cover with aluminum foil.

Bake for 30 minutes.

Makes 4–6 servings.

# Hamburger Stroganoff

## INGREDIENTS

2 pounds ground beef

2 medium onions

1 (8-ounce) can mushrooms, drained (reserve liquid)

1 (10.5-ounce) can cream of mushroom soup

1 (10.75-ounce) can tomato soup

1 teaspoon salt

2 cups sour cream

Hot cooked rice, noodles, or potatoes

## DIRECTIONS

Brown ground beef in a large skillet over medium heat. Drain and remove to a bowl. In same pan, cook onions in mushroom juice. Drain and return onion mixture to pan. Stir in mushrooms, soups, salt, and beef; simmer 5–10 minutes. Stir in sour cream and gently heat for a few minutes (don't boil). Serve over rice, noodles, or potatoes.

Makes 8–10 servings.

# Pot Roast Supreme

**INGREDIENTS**

1 beef roast (about 3 pounds)

All-purpose flour

2 tablespoons vegetable oil

6 carrots, peeled

6 potatoes, peeled

1 (10.5-ounce) can French onion soup

**DIRECTIONS**

Preheat oven to 275°.

Dredge roast in flour, and brown in oil in a skillet over medium heat. Transfer to a large baking dish. Arrange carrots and potatoes around roast. Heat soup in a saucepan, and pour over top.

Bake, covered, for 4 hours.

Makes 6 servings.


# Beef Brisket

**INGREDIENTS**

3–4 pounds beef brisket, rinsed and patted dry

3 tablespoons apple cider vinegar

Dash of Accent seasoning (optional)

1 teaspoon Lawry's seasoned salt

1 teaspoon paprika

1 teaspoon garlic salt

1 onion, sliced

2 cups hot water

**DIRECTIONS**

Preheat oven to 350°.

Place beef in a Dutch oven or roasting pan. Sprinkle vinegar and next 5 ingredients on top of meat.

Bake, uncovered, for 1 hour. Add 2 cups hot water. Cover, and bake 3–4 more hours. Cut into thin slices before serving.

Makes 6–10 servings.

# Barbecued Beef Brisket

*Start this recipe a few days ahead.*

## INGREDIENTS

6 pounds beef brisket

Garlic, onion and/or celery salt, to taste

3 tablespoons liquid smoke

Salt

Pepper

Worcestershire sauce

1 (18-ounce) bottle barbecue sauce

All-purpose flour (optional)

## DIRECTIONS

Sprinkle all sides of brisket with flavored salts. Place brisket in glass baking dish. Pour liquid smoke on meat. Cover and refrigerate overnight or up to several days.

Preheat oven to 250°.

Before baking, again sprinkle meat with flavored salts, plus salt, pepper, and Worcestershire sauce to taste.

Bake, covered, for 5 hours. Cut into thin slices. Add barbecue sauce. Bake for 1½ more hours. Thicken sauce with flour, if desired.

Makes 12–15 servings.

# Salisbury Steak

## INGREDIENTS

2 pounds ground beef

½ cup breadcrumbs

3 tablespoons minced fresh onion or
    2 teaspoons onion flakes

1 egg

2 teaspoons salt

½ teaspoon pepper

## DIRECTIONS

Preheat oven to 350°.

Mix together all ingredients in a large bowl. Portion and shape into 8 steaks; place in a baking dish.

Bake 30–45 minutes or until cooked through and no longer pink inside.

Makes 8 servings.

# Grilled Flank Steak

## INGREDIENTS

1½–2 pounds flank steak

¼ cup soy sauce

3 tablespoons honey

½ teaspoon ground ginger

½ cup vegetable oil

2 tablespoons vinegar

½ teaspoon garlic powder

## DIRECTIONS

Lightly score flank steak across the grain. Stir together soy sauce and next 5 ingredients in a covered glass baking dish or a zip-top plastic bag. Add steak, and marinate in the refrigerator for 24 to 48 hours.

Remove steak, and discard marinade. Grill 5–7 minutes per side. Cut, across the grain, into thin slices.

Makes 3–6 servings.

**Note:** Place steak in marinade in an airtight container, and pack it in a cooler before you leave. Serve with baked potatoes and coleslaw.

# Cheese-Stuffed Patties

## INGREDIENTS

1 pound ground beef

½ teaspoon salt

Dash of pepper

American cheese, shredded

Minced onion

Bottled barbecue sauce

## DIRECTIONS

Combine ground beef, salt, and pepper in a large bowl. Form into 6 (¼-inch-thick) patties on a sheet of wax paper. Place a small amount of cheese, onion, and barbecue sauce in the center of 3 patties. Top with remaining 3 meat patties. Press around edges to seal.

Grill over medium heat for about 8 minutes on each side.

Makes 3 servings.

# Florida Pork Chops

## INGREDIENTS

4 pork chops

1 cup orange juice

¼ cup brown sugar

1 teaspoon salt

1 teaspoon dry mustard

¼ teaspoon freshly ground pepper
or lemon pepper

## DIRECTIONS

Preheat oven to 350°.

Place chops in an 8-inch-square baking dish. Mix together orange juice and next 4 ingredients. Pour over top of chops. Add more orange juice, if needed, to cover.

Bake for 1¼ hours.

Makes 4 servings.

# Hinds Lake Fish with Sesame Butter

## INGREDIENTS

2 pounds northern pike or walleye fillets

½ teaspoon salt

¼ teaspoon pepper

½ cup butter, divided

4 tablespoons fresh lemon juice

Dash of Worcestershire sauce

6 tablespoons toasted sesame seeds

## GARNISH

Lemon quarters, fresh parsley

## DIRECTIONS

Preheat oven to 350°.

Arrange fish in a well-buttered shallow baking dish. Season with salt and pepper. Melt ¼ cup butter in a small saucepan over low heat. Brush fish with melted butter.

Bake for 20 minutes or until fish flakes easily when tested with a fork.

Heat remaining ¼ cup butter until it just starts to brown. Add lemon juice and Worcestershire sauce. Stir in sesame seeds. Spoon over baked fish. Garnish, if desired.

Makes 6 servings.

# Joe's Crappies

**INGREDIENTS**

Salt

Crappie fillets

Soda crackers

All-purpose flour

Butter

Vegetable oil

**DIRECTIONS**

Salt both sides of fillets and let them rest awhile. Meanwhile, crush soda crackers in a zip-top plastic bag. Add some flour to bag of crumbs, if desired. Drop fillets into plastic bag, and shake well to coat.

Heat vegetable oil in a large skillet over medium heat. Fry fillets quickly until tender. Place on paper towels to drain.

# Fish Fillets Almondine

**INGREDIENTS**

Fish fillets (walleye, northern pike, or bass)

2 tablespoons butter per fillet

1 teaspoon lemon juice per fillet

Paprika

Lemon pepper

Fine breadcrumbs

Sliced or slivered almonds

**DIRECTIONS**

Preheat to 450°.

Arrange fillets in a 9x9-inch baking dish. Melt butter in a small saucepan over low heat; stir in lemon juice. Pour over fillets, covering completely. Sprinkle with paprika, lemon pepper, and breadcrumbs.

Bake 8–15 minutes or until fish flakes easily with a fork. Sprinkle with almonds in the last 2 minutes. Watch carefully.

# Honey-Fried Walleye Fillets

## INGREDIENTS

6 large walleye fillets

⅔ cup vegetable oil

1 egg, lightly beaten

1 teaspoon honey

1½ cups coarsely crushed soda crackers

½ cup all-purpose flour

½ teaspoon salt

½ teaspoon pepper

## DIRECTIONS

Dry fillets on paper towels. Heat oil in a 10-inch skillet over medium heat.

Combine egg and honey in a bowl. In a separate bowl or zip-top plastic bag, combine cracker crumbs, flour, salt, and pepper. Dip fillets in honey mixture and then coat with cracker mixture, pressing crumbs firmly into fillets.

Fry about 3 minutes on each side in preheated oil.

Makes 6 servings.


# Easy Baked Fish

## INGREDIENTS

5 tablespoons butter

12–14 whole cleaned, scaled panfish, fresh or frozen

1 (10.5-ounce) can cream of celery soup

½ cup lemon juice

¼ cup dried parsley

## DIRECTIONS

Preheat oven to 350°.

Melt butter in a 9x13-inch baking dish. Arrange fish in butter. Pour soup and lemon juice over fish; sprinkle with parsley.

Bake for 50 minutes or until fish flakes easily with a fork.

Makes 6 servings.

# Caesar's Fillets

## INGREDIENTS

1 pound fish fillets

½ cup Caesar salad dressing

½ cup seasoned breadcrumbs

½ cup shredded cheddar cheese

## DIRECTIONS

Dry fish fillets well. Dip in Caesar dressing, and place in the bottom of a microwave-safe baking dish. Cover with breadcrumbs. Top with cheddar cheese. Cover.

Microwave on high for 5 minutes or until fish flakes easily with a fork. Let stand 1 minute. Check again.

Makes 3 servings.

# Sweet and Sour Chicken Wings

## INGREDIENTS

20–25 chicken wings

1 cup soy sauce

1 cup pineapple juice

1 teaspoon garlic powder

1 cup water

1 cup sugar

¼ cup vegetable oil

1 teaspoon ground ginger

## DIRECTIONS

Cut each wing in half, and cut off and discard tips. Place wings in shallow baking dish. Combine soy sauce and next 6 ingredients. Cover and refrigerate for at least 1 hour (overnight is better).

Preheat oven to 350°.

Remove wings from sauce and place on baking sheet. Bake, uncovered, 1–1¼ hours or until brown and tender.

Makes 8 servings.

**Note:** Serve these hot or cold as an appetizer. Pack them in the cooler and take them along. They'll keep in the refrigerator for several days.

# Glazed Chicken

## INGREDIENTS

1 (3-pound) package cut-up bone-in chicken or 4 split chicken breasts

1 (8-ounce) bottle Russian dressing

1 cup apricot preserves or orange marmalade

1 package dry onion soup mix

## DIRECTIONS

Preheat oven to 350°.

Place chicken in the bottom of a baking dish. Combine dressing, preserves, and soup mix in a bowl, and pour mixture over chicken.

Bake, uncovered, 1–1½ hours or until fork-tender. Baste with pan juices occasionally while baking.

Makes 4 servings.

# Tarragon Chicken

## INGREDIENTS

½ cup butter

2 (3-pound) packages cut-up bone-in chicken

4 teaspoons salt, divided

1 teaspoon pepper, divided

1 tablespoon paprika, divided

1 tablespoon chili powder, divided

2 teaspoons dried tarragon, divided

## DIRECTIONS

Preheat broiler.

Melt butter in a shallow baking dish. Place chicken, skin side down, in baking dish. Sprinkle with half of the salt, pepper, paprika, chili powder, and tarragon.

Place under broiler, about 5 inches from heat. Broil for about 15 minutes. Turn pieces over, and sprinkle with remaining salt, pepper, paprika, chili powder, and tarragon. Broil again for 15 minutes. Remove from broiler, and cover pan tightly with aluminum foil. Reduce oven temperature to 325°.

Bake 25–30 minutes.

Makes 8–10 servings.

# Honey Chicken

## INGREDIENTS

1 (3-pound) package cut-up
  bone-in chicken

4 tablespoons butter

½ cup honey

¼ cup mustard

1 teaspoon salt

1 teaspoon curry powder

## DIRECTIONS

Preheat oven to 375°.

Wash and dry chicken. Remove skin, if desired. Melt butter in a glass bowl in the microwave, and stir in honey, mustard, salt, and curry powder. Roll chicken in mixture to coat. Arrange, meaty side up, in a single layer in a baking dish. Cover with remaining sauce.

Bake for 1 hour or until chicken is tender and glazed.

Makes 4 servings.


# Chinese Chicken

## INGREDIENTS

⅓ cup soy sauce

2 tablespoons vegetable oil

1 teaspoon dry mustard

½ teaspoon ginger

¼ teaspoon pepper

1 clove garlic, minced

1 (3-pound) package cut-up
  bone-in chicken

## DIRECTIONS

Preheat oven to 375°.

Combine soy sauce and next 5 ingredients in a small bowl. Place washed and dried chicken parts in a large baking dish; brush with sauce. Let stand 30 minutes, and again brush with sauce.

Bake for about 50 minutes, brushing with sauce every 15 minutes.

Makes 4 servings.

**Note:** The drippings may be used as gravy on potatoes or biscuits. The sauce may be made ahead of time and stored in a jar.

# Parmesan Chicken

### INGREDIENTS

2 (3-pound) packages cut-up bone-in chicken

1 cup butter, melted

2 cups Italian-seasoned breadcrumbs

1 cup grated Parmesan cheese

¼ teaspoon instant minced garlic

½ teaspoon salt

2 tablespoons parsley flakes

### DIRECTIONS

Preheat oven to 375°.

Remove skin from chicken pieces. Melt butter in a small saucepan over low heat. Combine breadcrumbs and next 4 ingredients in a large bowl. Dip chicken pieces in butter, and roll in breadcrumb mixture. Arrange in a baking dish.

Bake, uncovered, for 1 hour.

Makes 8–10 servings.

# Delicious Easy Chicken

### INGREDIENTS

6–8 boneless skinless chicken breasts

1 (10.5-ounce) can cream of mushroom soup

½ cup sour cream

¼ cup mayonnaise

¼ cup dry white vermouth

Hot cooked white or wild rice

### DIRECTIONS

Preheat oven to 250°.

Place chicken in a lightly greased 9x13-inch baking dish. Combine soup, sour cream, mayonnaise, and vermouth in a small bowl. Pour over chicken breasts.

Bake, uncovered, 2½–3 hours. Serve over rice.

Makes 6–8 servings.

Vegetables
&
Side Dishes

# Dilly Beans

## INGREDIENTS

Fresh green beans

½ cup white vinegar

½ cup water

¼–½ cup sugar, to taste

1 teaspoon dry dill weed or 3 heads fresh dill

## DIRECTIONS

Wash beans and trim ends. Cut into pieces, if desired. Boil in unsalted water to cover in a large saucepan over high heat for 3 to 5 minutes until just tender. Drain beans, and put in ice water to stop the cooking process.

Drain cooled beans, and put in a large bowl. Mix together vinegar, ½ cup water, sugar, and dill weed in a separate bowl. Pour over beans, and stir to combine. Store in a covered container in the refrigerator.

 **Note:** This relish keeps in the refrigerator for several weeks.

# German Green Beans

## INGREDIENTS

2 slices bacon, cut up

1 (14.5-ounce) can green beans, mostly drained

1 green onion, chopped (including top) or onion powder

1 tablespoon vinegar

Parmesan cheese

## DIRECTIONS

Cook bacon in a large skillet over medium heat (do not drain). Add beans to bacon and drippings. Add onion and vinegar. Heat thoroughly. Transfer to a serving bowl, and sprinkle with Parmesan cheese.

Makes 3 servings.

# Bestemor's Baked Beans for a Crowd

## INGREDIENTS
1 pound bacon, cut into small pieces

1½ pounds ground beef

3 (28-ounce) cans Bush's baked beans

3 (4-ounce) cans mushrooms, drained

1½ cups ketchup

1 cup brown sugar

2 teaspoons dry mustard

## DIRECTIONS
Preheat oven to 325°.

Cook bacon in a large skillet over medium heat; remove to drain on paper towels, reserving drippings in skillet. Brown beef in drippings; drain and return to skillet. Stir in bacon, beans, mushrooms, ketchup, brown sugar, and dry mustard. Transfer to a baking dish.

Bake for about 1 hour or until thoroughly heated.

Makes 18–20 servings.

 **Note:** This can also be heated in a slow cooker for 4 hours or longer.

# Easy Baked Beans

## INGREDIENTS
1 teaspoon dry mustard

¾ cup brown sugar

2 (15-ounce) cans pork and beans

½ cup ketchup

6 slices bacon, cut up

## DIRECTIONS
Preheat oven to 325°.

Mix dry mustard and brown sugar together in a small bowl. Place beans in a baking dish, and sprinkle mustard mixture over top. Pour ketchup over top. Sprinkle with bacon pieces.

Cover and bake 2–3 hours.

Makes 6–8 servings.

# Broccoli Supreme

## INGREDIENTS

2 (10-ounce) packages frozen chopped broccoli or 2–3 heads of fresh broccoli, chopped

1 (10.5-ounce) can cream of chicken soup

2 carrots, peeled and grated

½ cup (4 ounces) sour cream

½ (2.8-ounce) can French's crispy fried onions or croutons

## DIRECTIONS

Preheat oven to 350°.

Bring water to a boil in a large saucepan. Add broccoli, return to a boil, and boil 3–4 minutes. Drain and allow to cool slightly.

Combine soup and next 3 ingredients in a large bowl; stir in broccoli. Transfer to a lightly greased baking dish.

Bake for 30 minutes.

Makes 6–8 servings.

# Baked Corn

## INGREDIENTS

1 (14.75-ounce) can cream-style corn

1 (15.25-ounce) can whole kernel corn, drained

1 egg, beaten

½ cup breadcrumbs or cracker crumbs

½ cup sour cream

½ teaspoon salt

Dash of pepper

## DIRECTIONS

Preheat oven to 350°.

Combine all ingredients in a large bowl. Transfer to a buttered baking dish.

Bake for about 40 minutes or until firm.

Makes 6 servings.

# Hot Fruit Compote

## INGREDIENTS

1 (15-ounce) can apricot halves, drained and quartered

1 (15-ounce) can sliced peaches, drained and quartered

1 (20-ounce) can pineapple chunks, drained

1 (14.5-ounce) jar apple rings, drained and quartered

1 (15.25-ounce) can pear halves, drained and quartered

½ cup butter

½ cup sugar

2 tablespoons all-purpose flour

1 cup golden sherry

## DIRECTIONS

Arrange apricot halves and next 4 ingredients in 9x13-inch baking dish. Heat butter, sugar, and flour in a saucepan over medium heat until thickened (cream consistency). Stir in sherry. Pour over fruit, cover, and let stand in refrigerator at least 8 hours or up to 24 hours.

Preheat oven to 350°.

Bake, covered, for 25 minutes; uncover and bake 5–10 more minutes. Serve immediately.

Makes 12 servings.

 **Note:** This keeps up to one week in the refrigerator after baking.

# Cauliflower and Carrots

## INGREDIENTS

1 small head cauliflower, broken into small pieces

2–3 carrots, peeled and sliced

1 (10.5-ounce) can cream of chicken soup

2 cups grated cheddar cheese

1 cup breadcrumbs

## DIRECTIONS

Preheat oven to 350°.

Cook cauliflower and carrots, in water to cover, in a saucepan over medium-high heat until just tender. In a lightly greased 2-quart baking dish, layer half each of the vegetables, soup, and cheese. Repeat layers. Cover top with breadcrumbs.

Bake, uncovered, for 30 minutes or until bubbly.

Makes 6 servings.

# Carrot-Cheese-Rice Casserole

## INGREDIENTS

2 cups cooked rice

2½ cups peeled, grated carrots

1½ cups shredded Colby or cheddar cheese

2 eggs, beaten

¼ cup milk

1 tablespoon butter, softened

¼ cup chopped onion

1 teaspoon salt

⅛ teaspoon pepper

## DIRECTIONS

Preheat oven to 350°.

Combine all ingredients in a large bowl. Transfer to a 1½-quart baking dish.

Bake for 45 minutes to 1 hour or until carrots are done.

Makes 4–6 servings.

# Carrots with Apples and Honey

## INGREDIENTS
1 pound carrots

1 teaspoon salt

1 teaspoon lemon juice

⅔ cup honey

1¾ cups diced apples

## DIRECTIONS
Peel carrots, split into halves, and slice about ¼-inch thick. Place carrots in a saucepan and cover with water. Boil gently until tender. Reserve 2 tablespoons of the boiling water, then drain carrots and place in a bowl; set aside. Return 2 tablespoons reserved water to saucepan, and add salt, lemon juice, and honey. Add diced apples.

Simmer gently for about 10 minutes. Add carrots. Simmer until apples are tender, about 5 more minutes.

Makes 4–6 servings.

# Granny's Grits

## INGREDIENTS
1 cup quick-cooking grits

4 cups water

1½ teaspoons salt

½ cup butter

1 cup shredded Longhorn or Colby cheese, divided

4 eggs, lightly beaten

1 cup milk

Dash of pepper

## DIRECTIONS
Preheat oven to 350°.

Cook grits in 4 cups water with salt according to package directions. Add butter and ¾ cup cheese to grits. Let cool slightly. Add eggs, milk, and pepper. Stir until well blended. Pour mixture into a 1½-quart baking dish. Top with remaining ¼ cup cheese.

Bake 45–60 minutes.

Makes 4–6 servings.

# Fried Green Tomatoes

## INGREDIENTS

4 medium-size green tomatoes, cut into thick slices

½ cup all-purpose flour

4 tablespoons bacon drippings or vegetable oil

Dash of salt

Dash of pepper

## DIRECTIONS

Dredge tomato slices in flour. Fry in hot drippings in a large skillet over medium heat, turning to brown both sides. Sprinkle with salt and pepper.

Makes 4 servings.

# Zucchini Casserole

## INGREDIENTS

3 pounds zucchini

3 onions, chopped

½ pound fresh mushrooms or 1 (4-ounce) can sliced mushrooms, drained

½ cup (1 stick) butter

### SAUCE

2 tablespoons butter

½ cup grated cheddar cheese

1 teaspoon seasoned salt

1 cup sour cream

### TOPPINGS

2 tablespoons grated cheddar cheese

Crushed Ritz crackers

## DIRECTIONS

Preheat oven to 350°.

Slice zucchini into thin slices. Parboil in a saucepan in salted water to cover until just tender, about 3 minutes. Drain, then rinse under cold water to stop the cooking process. Drain.

In a large skillet, sauté onions and fresh mushrooms in ½ cup butter until onions and mushrooms have softened and mushrooms have given up some liquid. (If using canned mushrooms, add after onions are soft and only sauté until heated through.)

To make sauce, melt 2 tablespoons butter in a large saucepan over medium heat. Stir in cheese, seasoned salt, and sour cream. Add zucchini and onion-mushroom mixture, and heat through. Pour into a 1½- or 2-quart baking dish.

Sprinkle 2 tablespoons cheese and crushed crackers over all.

Bake, uncovered, for 30 minutes.

Makes 8 servings.

# Easy Rice Casserole

## INGREDIENTS

1½ cups uncooked white rice

1 (10.5-ounce) can beef consommé

1 (10.5-ounce) can French onion soup

1 (8-ounce) can sliced mushrooms, undrained

½ cup (1 stick) butter

⅓ cup Parmesan cheese

## DIRECTIONS

Preheat oven to 350°.

Combine all ingredients in a large bowl, and transfer to a baking dish.

Bake, uncovered, for 1 hour. Stir occasionally. (For a double recipe, bake about 1 hour and 25 minutes or until liquid is absorbed.)

Makes 6–8 servings.

# Noodles and Rice Casserole

## INGREDIENTS

½ cup butter

8 ounces uncooked fine egg noodles

2 cups uncooked Minute Rice

2 (10.5-ounce) cans French onion soup

2 (10.5-ounce) cans chicken broth

4 tablespoons soy sauce

1 (8-ounce) can sliced water chestnuts, drained

1 (4-ounce) can sliced mushrooms, drained (optional)

## DIRECTIONS

Preheat oven to 350°.

Melt butter in a large skillet over medium heat. Add noodles. Cook until lightly browned, stirring constantly. Add rice, next 4 ingredients, and, if desired, mushrooms. Mix well. Transfer to a 3-quart baking dish.

Bake, uncovered, for 45 minutes, stirring occasionally.

Makes 10–12 servings.

# Wild Rice Casserole

**INGREDIENTS**

1 cup uncooked wild rice

½ medium-size onion, chopped

2 tablespoons butter

3 chicken bouillon cubes

¼ cup hot water

1 (10.5-ounce) can cream of mushroom soup

1 soup can of water

2 (4-ounce) cans mushrooms, drained

**DIRECTIONS**

Preheat oven to 325°.

Wash and drain rice. Sauté onion in butter in a skillet over medium heat. Dissolve chicken bouillon cubes in ¼ cup hot water. Add rice, bouillon mixture, soup, soup can of water, and mushrooms to skillet. Transfer mixture to a baking dish.

Cover, and bake 1½–2 hours. Do not overcook.

Makes 4–6 servings.

 **Note:** Add ¼–1 pound browned ground beef to make a main dish. This recipe freezes well.

# Rice and Fresh Mushrooms

**INGREDIENTS**

½ cup butter, melted

1½ cups uncooked white rice

1 (10.5-ounce) can beef consommé

1 (10.5-ounce) can French onion soup

8 ounces fresh mushrooms, cleaned and sliced

8 ounces (2 cups) shredded sharp cheddar cheese

**DIRECTIONS**

Preheat oven to 350°.

Melt butter in a saucepan over medium heat. Add rice, soups, and mushrooms. Mix and heat through. Pour into a 7x11-inch baking dish.

Cover, and bake for about 1 hour. Uncover, and sprinkle with cheese for the last few minutes of baking.

Makes 6 servings.

# Sliced Baked Potatoes

**INGREDIENTS**

Baking potatoes (1 per person)

Butter (about 4 tablespoons for a 9x13-inch pan)

Salt, to taste

Parmesan cheese (optional)

**DIRECTIONS**

Preheat oven to 400°.

Peel potatoes. Slice lengthwise into ¼-inch-thick slices. Melt butter in a baking dish in the oven. Put potatoes in dish, and turn to coat with butter.

Bake for 30 minutes. Sprinkle with salt and, if desired, Parmesan cheese before serving.

# Sunshine Lemon Potatoes

**INGREDIENTS**

3 large potatoes, thinly sliced

¼ cup melted butter

1 tablespoon fresh lemon juice

2 teaspoons freshly grated lemon zest

3 tablespoons Parmesan cheese or seasoned croutons

½ teaspoon paprika

**DIRECTIONS**

Preheat oven to 350°.

Arrange potatoes in 9x13-inch baking dish. Combine butter and lemon juice in a small bowl. Brush mixture over potatoes. Combine lemon zest, Parmesan cheese, and paprika in a small bowl. Sprinkle over potatoes.

Bake for 45 minutes.

Makes 4 servings.

# Scalloped Potatoes

## INGREDIENTS

Sliced raw potatoes

Whipping cream

Salt and pepper

Parmesan cheese (optional)

## DIRECTIONS

Preheat oven to 350°.

Layer potatoes in a baking dish; sprinkle generously with salt and pepper. Combine equal parts whipping cream and water in small bowl; pour mixture over potatoes, covering about two-thirds the depth of potatoes. Sprinkle with Parmesan cheese, if desired.

Bake, uncovered, for about 1 hour or until done.

# Mashed Potato Casserole

## INGREDIENTS

5 pounds red potatoes

1 (8-ounce) package cream cheese, softened

1 cup half-and-half

½ cup (1 stick) butter, melted and divided

1 teaspoon salt

1 teaspoon onion salt

¼ teaspoon paprika

## DIRECTIONS

Peel potatoes, and halve or quarter any large ones. Boil in large saucepan in enough water to cover until just tender; drain.

Preheat oven to 350°.

Combine cream cheese with half-and-half in a large bowl, beating until well blended. Add well-drained potatoes. Mash, blending well. Add melted butter (reserving 1 tablespoon), and then add salt and onion salt. Transfer to a 2-quart baking dish. Brush with reserved 1 tablespoon butter. Sprinkle with paprika.

Bake for 30 minutes.

Makes 12–15 servings.

**Note:** Recipe can be refrigerated for later baking; bake at 350° for 45 minutes.

# Potato Casserole

## INGREDIENTS

3 cups half-and-half

1 cup milk

½ cup (1 stick) butter, melted and cooled

⅔ cup Parmesan cheese

1 teaspoon salt

2 pounds Ore Ida diced hash brown potatoes

## DIRECTIONS

Preheat oven to 325°.

Combine half-and-half, milk, and cooled butter in a large bowl. Mix in cheese, salt, and hash browns. Transfer to a 2-quart glass baking dish.

Bake, covered, for 45 minutes. Uncover and bake 15 more minutes.

Makes 6–8 servings.

# Vermicelli in a Skillet

## INGREDIENTS

1 cup (2 sticks) butter

⅔ (16-ounce) package uncooked vermicelli

1 cup uncooked Minute Rice

2 (10.5-ounce) cans French onion soup

½ soup can of water

1 cup sliced mushrooms, undrained

4 green onions, chopped (tops included)

## DIRECTIONS

Melt butter in a large skillet over medium heat. Add vermicelli, and cook until lightly browned. Add rice, and brown a little longer. Stir in soup and next 3 ingredients.

Cover, and simmer for 20 minutes. Uncover, and cook a little longer, if needed, until all the liquid is absorbed.

Makes 8 servings.

# Desserts

# Red Grape Dessert

### INGREDIENTS

¼ cup sour cream

¼ cup cream cheese, softened

2 tablespoons sugar

1 pound seedless red grapes

### DIRECTIONS

Combine sour cream, cream cheese, and sugar in a large bowl. Fold in grapes. Refrigerate for a few hours before serving in small bowls.

Serves 4–6.

 **Note:** This keeps well for a few days in the refrigerator.

# Fresh Fruit Compote

### INGREDIENTS

Fresh fruit (such as peaches, nectarines, blueberries, strawberries, cantaloupe, honeydew, grapes, and watermelon)

Sugar

¼ cup orange liqueur or kirsch (optional)

### DIRECTIONS

Prepare a variety of fresh, seasonal fruit. Arrange in layers in a glass bowl, sprinkling sugar lightly over each layer. Spoon liqueur over each layer for flavor, if desired. Toss gently, and chill for at least 2 hours.

# Cantaloupe with Blueberry Yogurt

**INGREDIENTS**

1 cantaloupe, halved and seeded

Blueberry yogurt

**DIRECTIONS**

Cut cantaloupe into 8–10 wedges. Top each wedge with a generous dollop of blueberry yogurt.

Makes 8–10 servings.

# Frozen Grapes

**INGREDIENTS**

Green or red seedless grapes

**DIRECTIONS**

Wash grapes and remove stems. Drain on paper towels. Freeze in a single layer on a baking sheet. When frozen, transfer to a large zip-top plastic bag or airtight container.

# Orange Strawberry Dessert

## INGREDIENTS

½ (12-ounce) can frozen orange juice concentrate, thawed

¾ cup sugar

1 pint strawberries, washed, hulled, and halved

6 oranges, peeled and sectioned

## DIRECTIONS

Mix concentrate and sugar together in a large bowl. Let stand several minutes, until sugar is dissolved. Combine strawberries and orange sections in another bowl. Pour concentrate mixture over fruit. Mix well. Refrigerate several hours or overnight.

Makes 6 servings.

# Heavenly Summer Fruit Delight

## INGREDIENTS

Fresh fruit (such as raspberries, blueberries, strawberries, and peaches)

Sour Cream

Brown sugar

## DIRECTIONS

Place fruit in individual serving dishes. Spoon a dollop of cold sour cream (about 1 heaping tablespoon per serving) on top. Sprinkle generously with brown sugar.

# Frozen Fruit Cups

## INGREDIENTS

2 (10-ounce) packages frozen strawberries, thawed

1 (15-ounce) can apricot halves, drained and cut up

1 (20-ounce) can crushed pineapple, undrained

4 bananas, diced

### SYRUP

2 cups sugar

1 cup water

## DIRECTIONS

Combine strawberries and next 3 ingredients.

To make syrup, bring sugar and water to a boil in a large saucepan over medium-high heat until sugar dissolves. Cool. Pour over mixed fruit. Ladle into individual serving dishes, such as paper soufflé cups or 5-ounce plastic glasses. Freeze. Cover with aluminum foil when frozen. Remove from freezer 35–45 minutes before serving.

Makes 15–25 servings.

# Blueberry-Green Grape Combo

## INGREDIENTS

¾ cup sour cream

¼ cup brown sugar

2 cups blueberries

2 cups green grapes

### GARNISH

Brown sugar

## DIRECTIONS

Combine sour cream and brown sugar in a large bowl. Add blueberries and grapes, tossing to coat. Divide into 4 serving dishes. Garnish, if desired. Chill before serving.

Makes 4 servings.

# Orange Take-Along Cake

## INGREDIENTS

1¼ cups boiling water

1 cup quick-cooking oats

½ cup butter, softened

1 cup granulated sugar

½ cup brown sugar

2 eggs

½ cup frozen orange juice concentrate, thawed

1 teaspoon vanilla extract

1¾ cups all-purpose flour

1 teaspoon baking powder

1 teaspoon baking soda

½ teaspoon salt

½ teaspoon cinnamon

½ cup chopped walnuts

## DIRECTIONS

Preheat oven to 350°.

In a small bowl, pour 1¼ cups boiling water over oats. Set aside. In a large bowl, cream butter and sugars. Beat in eggs, one at a time. Add orange juice concentrate and vanilla.

In a medium bowl, sift together flour and next 4 ingredients. Blend flour mixture into creamed mixture, alternating with oats, beginning and ending with flour mixture. Fold in walnuts. Pour into a greased 9x13-inch baking dish.

Bake for 40 minutes.

Makes 12–16 servings.

# Cheesecake

## INGREDIENTS

1¼ cups graham cracker crumbs

¼ cup butter, just barely melted

¾ cup sugar, divided

1 (8-ounce) package cream cheese, softened

1 tablespoon lemon juice

½ teaspoon vanilla extract

⅛ teaspoon salt

2 eggs, beaten

1 cup sour cream

½ teaspoon vanilla extract

## DIRECTIONS

Preheat oven to 350°.

Combine cracker crumbs, butter, and 2 tablespoons sugar in a bowl. Pat into an 8-inch pie plate or 8-inch-square baking dish. Combine cream cheese, ½ cup sugar, lemon juice, vanilla, salt, and eggs in a large bowl; mix well. Pour into prepared crust.

Bake 25–30 minutes.

Mix sour cream, remaining 2 tablespoons sugar, and vanilla in a small bowl. Pour over hot, baked cheesecake. Bake 10 more minutes. Cool. Refrigerate or freeze.

Makes 8 servings.

# Strawberry Cheesecake

## INGREDIENTS

2½ cups graham cracker crumbs

½ cup (1 stick) butter, just barely melted

1¼ cups sugar, divided

1 (3-ounce) package strawberry gelatin mix

1 cup boiling water

1 (10-ounce) package frozen strawberries

1 (8-ounce) package cream cheese, softened

1 (12-ounce) can evaporated milk, chilled

## GARNISH

Fresh strawberries

## DIRECTIONS

Combine cracker crumbs, butter, and ¼ cup sugar in a small bowl. Pat into a 9x13-inch baking dish. In a large bowl, dissolve gelatin in 1 cup boiling water. Add frozen strawberries. Set aside to cool. In a separate bowl, beat cream cheese and remaining 1 cup sugar until fluffy. In a separate chilled bowl, whip evaporated milk until it resembles whipped cream. Fold creamed mixture and whipped cream into strawberry mixture, and pour into prepared crust.

Chill in refrigerator for several hours. Garnish, if desired.

Makes 12 servings.

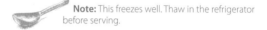 **Note:** This freezes well. Thaw in the refrigerator before serving.

# Individual Cherry Cheesecakes

## INGREDIENTS

2 (8-ounce) packages cream cheese, softened

¾ cup sugar

2 eggs

1 teaspoon vanilla extract

24 vanilla wafers

1 can cherry pie filling

## DIRECTIONS

Preheat oven to 350°.

Beat cream cheese and sugar in a large bowl until creamy. Add eggs and vanilla; mix well. Place 24 muffin cup liners in muffin pans. Put a vanilla wafer in bottom of each. Spoon cheese mixture on top.

Bake for 20 minutes. Remove from pans, and cool. Top evenly with cherry pie filling. Chill overnight before serving.

Makes 24 servings.

 **Note:** These freeze well.

# Jiffy Shortcake

## INGREDIENTS

1 cup self-rising flour

1 cup vanilla ice cream, softened

## DIRECTIONS

Preheat oven to 400°.

Mix flour and ice cream. Drop by spoonfuls onto an ungreased baking sheet.

Bake for about 15 minutes or until light brown.

Makes 6 servings.

# Mandarin Orange Cake

## INGREDIENTS

2 (11-ounce) cans mandarin oranges

2 cups all-purpose flour

2 eggs

2 teaspoons baking soda

2 cups sugar

2 teaspoons vanilla extract

1 teaspoon salt

## GLAZE

1½ cups brown sugar

6 tablespoons butter

6 tablespoons milk

## GARNISH

Whipped cream

## DIRECTIONS

Preheat oven to 325°.

Remove excess liquid from oranges, but do not completely drain. Combine oranges and next 6 ingredients in a large bowl. Beat until well blended and oranges are broken up. Transfer to a lightly greased 9x13-inch cake pan.

Bake 30–35 minutes.

To make glaze, combine brown sugar, butter, and milk in a saucepan over high heat. Boil for 3 minutes, stirring constantly. Make holes in hot cake with fork. Pour hot glaze over cake. Garnish, if desired.

# Cranberry Bundt Cake

## INGREDIENTS

⅓ cup poppy seeds

1 cup warm water

1 (15.25-ounce) box yellow cake mix

1 (3.4-ounce) package instant vanilla pudding mix

½ cup vegetable oil

4 eggs

2 cups fresh cranberries, rinsed

## DIRECTIONS

Preheat oven to 350°.

Soak poppy seeds in 1 cup warm water in a large bowl for about 10 minutes; don't drain. Beat in cake mix and next 4 ingredients for 2 minutes with an electric mixer. Transfer batter to a well-greased tube or Bundt pan.

Bake 60–75 minutes. Cool cake in pan for 10 minutes. Remove cake to a wire rack to cool completely.

# Apple Cake

## INGREDIENTS

¼ cup butter

1 cup sugar

1 egg

1 cup all-purpose flour

1 teaspoon baking soda

½ teaspoon salt

¾ teaspoon cinnamon

2¼ cups peeled, coarsely grated apple

½ cup chopped nuts

½ cup raisins

2 teaspoons vanilla extract

Powdered sugar

Whipped topping (optional)

## DIRECTIONS

Preheat oven to 350°.

Cream butter, sugar, and egg in a large bowl. In a separate bowl, sift together flour, baking soda, salt, and cinnamon. Add flour mixture to creamed mixture in thirds, blending well after each addition. Stir in apple, nuts, raisins, and vanilla until thoroughly mixed. Spread into a lightly greased 8x8-inch baking dish.

Bake for 45 minutes or until a toothpick inserted in center comes out clean.

After cake has cooled slightly, sift powdered sugar over top. Serve with whipped topping, if desired.

Makes 9–12 servings.

# Lumberjack Chocolate Sheet Cake

## INGREDIENTS

2 cups granulated sugar

2 cups all-purpose flour

1 teaspoon salt

1 teaspoon baking soda

1 cup (2 sticks) butter

1 cup water

4 tablespoons cocoa

½ cup sour cream

2 eggs

## FROSTING

1 cup butter

6 tablespoons sweetened condensed milk

2 tablespoons cocoa

1 teaspoon vanilla extract

1 pound (3½ cups) powdered sugar, sifted

## DIRECTIONS

Preheat oven to 375°.

In a large bowl, mix granulated sugar, flour, salt, and baking soda. Combine 1 cup butter, 1 cup water, and 4 tablespoons cocoa in a medium saucepan over high heat. Bring to a boil. Stir chocolate mixture into flour mixture. Add sour cream and eggs, and mix to combine. Pour batter into a lightly greased 11x17-inch jelly roll pan. Bake 15–18 minutes.

To make frosting, combine 1 cup butter, condensed milk, 2 tablespoons cocoa, and vanilla in a medium saucepan over high heat. Bring to a boil. Add powdered sugar. Beat well. Allow frosting to cool, and spread over cooled cake.

Makes 20 servings.

# Date-Chocolate Picnic Cake

*This moist cake has a "baked-in" topping, and travels very well.*

## INGREDIENTS

1 cup chopped dates

1½ cups boiling water

1¾ teaspoons baking soda, divided

½ cup shortening

½ cup granulated sugar

1 cup brown sugar, divided

2 eggs

1¾ cups all-purpose flour

¼ teaspoon salt

6 ounces (¾ cup) semi-sweet
  chocolate chips

½ cup chopped nuts

## DIRECTIONS

Preheat oven to 350°.

In a small bowl, combine dates, 1½ cups boiling water, and 1 teaspoon baking soda; let cool. In a large bowl, cream shortening, granulated sugar, ½ cup brown sugar, and eggs. Add date mixture, and stir well. Add flour, salt, and remaining ¾ teaspoon baking soda, and mix to combine. Pour batter into a lightly greased 9x13-inch baking pan.

Combine chocolate chips, remaining ½ cup brown sugar, and nuts in a small bowl, and sprinkle over batter.

Bake for 30–40 minutes.

Makes 12 servings.

# Rhubarb Cake

## INGREDIENTS

½ cup shortening

1½ cups granulated sugar

1 egg, beaten

1 teaspoon vanilla extract

1 cup buttermilk

1 teaspoon baking soda

2 cups all-purpose flour

½ teaspoon salt

3–4 cups diced fresh rhubarb

### GLAZE

2 tablespoons butter, softened

3 tablespoons milk

1 cup powdered sugar, sifted

## DIRECTIONS

Preheat oven to 350°.

In a large bowl, cream shortening and sugar. Add egg. Stir in vanilla.

Pour buttermilk into a 2-cup container. Add baking soda, and mix. In a medium bowl, combine flour and salt. Add to creamed mixture, alternating with buttermilk mixture. Fold in rhubarb. Mix well.

Pour batter into a lightly greased and floured 9x13-inch baking pan.

Bake for 45 minutes.

To make glaze, combine butter, milk, and powdered sugar in a bowl. Spread on cooled cake.

Makes 16 servings.

# Mississippi Mud Cake

### INGREDIENTS

1 cup butter, melted

2 cups granulated sugar

⅓ cup cocoa

1½ cups all-purpose flour

4 eggs, beaten

1 cup coconut

1 cup pecans, coarsely chopped

1 (7-ounce) jar marshmallow crème

### FROSTING

6 tablespoons butter

1 square (1 ounce) unsweetened chocolate

¼ cup milk

3 cups powdered sugar

1 teaspoon vanilla extract

### DIRECTIONS

Preheat oven to 350°.

Add 1 cup butter and next 4 ingredients to a large bowl. Beat together by hand. Fold in coconut and pecans. Pour batter into a lightly greased 9x13-inch baking pan.

Bake for 40 minutes. Remove from oven, and immediately spread marshmallow crème over cake. Let cool.

To make frosting, melt 6 tablespoons butter in a saucepan over low heat; stir in chocolate and milk. Stir in powdered sugar and vanilla. Spread over marshmallow crème.

Makes 12–15 servings.

# Big Lake Cake

### INGREDIENTS

2 (21-ounce) cans blueberry pie filling

1 (15.25-ounce) box white cake mix

½ cup (1 stick) butter, melted

⅔ cup slivered almonds

### DIRECTIONS

Preheat oven to 350°.

Spread blueberry pie filling on bottom of a 9x13-inch buttered baking pan. Sprinkle dry cake mix on top. Drizzle melted butter over cake mix. Sprinkle almonds on top.

Bake for 50 minutes.

Makes 12–15 servings.

# Carrot Cake

## INGREDIENTS

2 cups granulated sugar

2 cups all-purpose flour

2 teaspoons baking soda

2 teaspoons baking powder

2 teaspoons cinnamon

1 teaspoon salt

4 eggs, beaten

1½ cups vegetable oil

3 cups shredded carrots

½ cup chopped pecans

1 teaspoon vanilla extract

## FROSTING

6 ounces cream cheese, softened

¼ cup (½ stick) butter, softened

1 pound (3½ cups) powdered sugar, sifted

2 teaspoons vanilla extract

## DIRECTIONS

Preheat oven to 300°.

Combine granulated sugar and next 5 ingredients in a large bowl. Add eggs, oil, carrots, pecans, and 1 teaspoon vanilla. Pour batter into a lightly greased 9x13-inch baking pan.

Bake for 1 hour. Check for doneness.

To make frosting, combine cream cheese and next 3 ingredients. Mix well. Spread on cooled cake.

Makes 16 servings.

# Cherry Crunch

### INGREDIENTS

1 (21-ounce) can cherry pie filling

¾ cup Bisquick

¼ cup butter, softened

½ cup sugar

½ cup chopped nuts

½ teaspoon cinnamon

### DIRECTIONS

Preheat oven to 350°.

Pour pie filling into an ungreased 9-inch-square baking pan. Combine Bisquick and next 4 ingredients in a small bowl, and sprinkle over pie filling. Bake for 25–30 minutes.

Makes 6–8 servings.

# Crazy Cherry Cake

### INGREDIENTS

¼ cup vegetable oil

1 (15.25-ounce) white cake mix

2 eggs

½ cup water

1 (21-ounce) can cherry pie filling

### CREAM CHEESE FROSTING

3 ounces cream cheese, softened

1 tablespoon milk

1 teaspoon lemon juice

Dash of salt

2½ cups powdered sugar, sifted

### DIRECTIONS

Preheat oven to 350°.

Spread oil around a 9x13-inch cake pan. Add cake mix, eggs, and ½ cup water, combining well. Add pie filling. Mix with batter just to marbleize.

Bake for about 30 minutes or until a knife inserted in center comes out clean.

To make frosting, combine cream cheese, milk, lemon juice, and salt in a large bowl. Gradually add powdered sugar, beating until smooth and spreading consistency. If too thick, stir in additional milk, 1 teaspoon at a time. Spread frosting on cooled cake.

Makes 12–15 servings.

# Nötkaka

*This nut cake recipe comes from Sweden, where they use hazelnuts.*

## INGREDIENTS

3 eggs

1 cup sugar

1 (6-ounce) package chopped hazelnuts, pecans, or walnuts

½ teaspoon baking powder

Whipped cream

## DIRECTIONS

Preheat oven to 350°.

Beat eggs and sugar in a large bowl. Add nuts and baking powder.

Pour batter into a well-greased and sugared 8x8-inch baking pan.

Bake for 40 minutes. Serve with whipped cream.

# Choc-Dot Pumpkin Cake or Cupcakes

## INGREDIENTS

2 cups all-purpose flour

2 teaspoons baking powder

1 teaspoon baking soda

½ teaspoon salt

1½ teaspoons cinnamon

½ teaspoon ground cloves

¼ teaspoon allspice

¼ teaspoon ground ginger

2 cups granulated sugar

4 eggs

1 (15-ounce) can pumpkin

1 cup vegetable oil

1 cup All Bran cereal

6-ounces (¾ cup) semi-sweet
   chocolate chips

1 cup chopped nuts

### LEMON GLAZE

2 tablespoons butter, softened

1½ cups powdered sugar

2 teaspoons lemon juice

2 tablespoons orange juice

## DIRECTIONS

Preheat oven to 350°.

Sift together flour and next 8 ingredients in a large bowl. In a separate large bowl, beat eggs until foamy. Add pumpkin, oil, and cereal. Mix well. Add flour mixture to pumpkin mixture, stirring until just combined. Stir in chocolate chips and nuts. Spoon batter into lightly greased mini-cupcake pans, filling two-thirds full.

Bake 20–25 minutes. Cool.

To make glaze, cream butter and next 3 ingredients. Pour over cupcakes.

Makes 100 mini-cupcakes.

**Note:** You can also bake this recipe in a tube pan for about 70 minutes. Cool completely before removing from pan. This recipe freezes well.

# Minnesota Sundae

**DIRECTIONS**

Top vanilla ice cream with honey and sunflower seeds.

# Berry Pie

**CRUST**

2 cups all-purpose flour

1¼ teaspoons salt

2 teaspoons sugar

⅔ cup vegetable oil

3 tablespoons milk

**FILLING**

4 cups fresh berries

1 cup sugar

¼ cup all-purpose flour

¼ teaspoon cinnamon

⅛ teaspoon nutmeg

⅛ teaspoon cloves

2 tablespoons butter

**DIRECTIONS**

Preheat oven to 400°.

To make crust, mix flour and next 4 ingredients together in an 8x8-inch baking pan. Reserve 1 cup flour mixture. Pat remaining flour mixture into bottom of pan.

To make filling, mix berries and next 5 ingredients together in a large bowl. Pour over prepared crust. Dot with butter. Sprinkle reserved flour mixture on top.

Bake 40–50 minutes.

Makes 9 servings.

 **Note:** This pie crust doesn't require a rolling pin.

# Easy Refrigerator Pie

## INGREDIENTS

½ (12-ounce) can frozen lemonade, thawed

1 (14-ounce) can sweetened condensed milk

1 (8-ounce) container non-dairy
   whipped topping

2 (8-ounce) cans crushed pineapple, drained

2–3 drops yellow food coloring (optional)

2 store-bought prepared graham
   cracker crusts

## DIRECTIONS

Combine lemonade and condensed milk in a large
bowl. Stir in whipped topping, pineapple, and, if
desired, food coloring; mix well. Divide mixture
between 2 piecrusts. Chill for at least 2 hours.

Makes 2 pies (12 servings).


# Chocolate Amaretto Pie

## INGREDIENTS

1½ cups Oreo cookie crumbs

¼ cup butter, softened

1 tablespoon sugar

⅓ cup plus 2 tablespoons amaretto
   liqueur, divided

1 quart chocolate ice cream, softened

1 cup whipping cream

## GARNISH

Chocolate sprinkles

## DIRECTIONS

Mix crumbs, butter, and sugar together in a bowl. Press
mixture into an ungreased 9-inch pie plate. Refrigerate
until completely chilled.

In a large bowl, stir ⅓ cup amaretto into ice cream. Pour
into chilled piecrust.

Mix cream and remaining 2 tablespoons amaretto in a
medium-size chilled bowl. Beat until stiff peaks form. Pile
whipped cream in mounds around edge of pie. Garnish,
if desired. Freeze. Take out 10 minutes before serving.

Makes 6–8 servings.

# Apple Crisp

**INGREDIENTS**

Apples, peeled, cored, and sliced

Dash of cinnamon

1 teaspoon salt

¼ cup water

1 cup all-purpose flour

1¼ cups sugar

½ cup butter

Vanilla ice cream

**DIRECTIONS**

Preheat oven to 350°.

Place enough apple slices in a buttered 9x13-inch baking pan to fill ¾ full. Sprinkle with cinnamon, salt, and ¼ cup water. Combine flour and sugar in a large bowl, and cut in butter with a pastry blender. Sprinkle flour mixture over apples.

Bake for 40 minutes. Serve warm with ice cream.

Makes 8–10 servings.

# No-Crust Pumpkin Pie

**INGREDIENTS**

4 eggs

¾ cup sugar

1 teaspoon ginger

1 teaspoon cinnamon

½ teaspoon salt

1 (15-ounce) can pumpkin

1 cup milk

**DIRECTIONS**

Preheat oven to 325°.

Beat eggs in a large bowl. Add sugar, ginger, cinnamon, and salt. Stir in pumpkin. Blend in milk, and stir until mixture is smooth. Pour into a lightly greased 9-inch pie plate.

Bake for 50 minutes or until firm, when knife inserted in filling 2 inches from center comes out clean.

# Apple Pie Pudding

## INGREDIENTS

2 large tart cooking apples, peeled, cored, and thinly sliced

¾ cup brown sugar, divided

½ cup self-rising flour

¼ cup butter, softened

½ cup chopped pecans

Whipped cream (optional)

## DIRECTIONS

Preheat oven to 350°.

Arrange half of the apple slices in a baking dish. Sprinkle with ¼ cup brown sugar. Repeat layers with remaining half apples and ¼ cup brown sugar. Mix together remaining ¼ cup brown sugar and flour in a small bowl. Cream in the butter. Add pecans. Spread creamed mixture on top of apples.

Bake for 45 minutes. Top with cream, if desired.

Makes 4 servings.

# Brown Rice Pudding

## INGREDIENTS

2 cups cooked brown rice

3 cups milk

3 eggs, beaten

¾ cup brown sugar or honey

1 cup raisins

Dash of nutmeg

Dash of cinnamon (optional)

Heavy cream

## DIRECTIONS

Preheat oven to 350°.

Combine rice, next 5 ingredients, and, if desired, cinnamon. Spread in a buttered 9x13-inch baking dish.

Bake for 1 hour. Serve with cream.

Makes 8–10 servings.

# Frozen Chocolate Cream Pie

### INGREDIENTS

1 (4-ounce) package Baker's German's sweet chocolate

⅓ cup milk, divided

2 tablespoons sugar

3 ounces cream cheese, softened

1 (8-ounce container) non-dairy whipped topping

1 (8-inch) store-bought graham cracker crust

### GARNISH

Chocolate curls

### DIRECTIONS

Heat chocolate and 2 tablespoons milk in a saucepan over low heat, stirring until chocolate is melted. In a large bowl, beat sugar into cream cheese. Add remaining 3 tablespoons milk and chocolate mixture. Beat until smooth. Fold in whipped topping, blending until smooth. Spoon into crust.

Freeze until firm, about 4 hours. Garnish, if desired. Remove from freezer 10 minutes before serving. Store any leftover pie in the freezer.

# Favorite Refrigerator Dessert

### INGREDIENTS

1 cup all-purpose flour

½ cup chopped nuts

½ cup butter

1 (8-ounce) package cream cheese, softened

1 cup powdered sugar

1 (8-ounce) container non-dairy whipped topping, divided

2 packages instant pudding mix (any flavor)

3 cups milk

Chopped roasted nuts

### DIRECTIONS

Preheat oven to 350°.

Mix together flour and nuts in a bowl. Cut in butter. Press flour mixture into an ungreased 9x13-inch baking pan. Bake for 15 minutes. Cool.

In a large bowl, blend cream cheese and powdered sugar. Add 1 cup whipped topping to creamed mixture. Spread over cooled crust. Beat together instant pudding mix and milk. Spread over cream cheese layer. Spread remaining whipped topping over pudding layer. Sprinkle with nuts. Refrigerate for several hours or overnight.

Makes 20 servings.

# Crème de Coffee Dessert

### INGREDIENTS

Coffee-flavored ice cream

Crème de cacao (liqueur or flavoring)

Roasted pecans or almonds, whole or chopped

### DIRECTIONS

Top each serving of ice cream with 2 tablespoons of crème de cacao. Sprinkle with nuts.


# Quick Summer Trifle

### INGREDIENTS

1 (9-ounce) package Jiffy white cake mix

Fresh fruit (such as peaches, strawberries, and blueberries)

1 package vanilla instant pudding mix

3 ounces cream cheese, softened

1 (8-ounce) carton non-dairy whipped topping or 1 cup whipping cream, whipped and sweetened

### DIRECTIONS

Preheat oven to 350°.

Prepare cake mix according to package directions. Pour batter into a 9x13-inch baking pan. Bake 15–25 minutes or until a toothpick inserted in the center comes out clean. When cooled, cover cake with a layer of sliced fresh fruit.

Prepare pudding according to package directions, and mix with cream cheese. Spread over fruit. Cover with whipped topping. Refrigerate.

Makes 12–15 servings.

# Schaum Torte

## MERINGUE CRUST

4 egg whites (reserve yolks for filling)

¼ teaspoon cream of tartar

1 cup granulated sugar

## FILLING

4 egg yolks, well beaten

½ cup granulated sugar

3 tablespoons fresh lemon juice

Zest of 1 lemon

## TOPPING

1 cup whipping cream

1 tablespoon powdered sugar

## DIRECTIONS

Preheat oven to 275°.

To make crust, beat egg whites in a large bowl until frothy. Add cream of tartar and continue to beat. Gradually add 1 cup granulated sugar, beating until stiff and glossy. Spread into a well-greased pie plate. Bake for 20 minutes; increase temperature to 300° and bake for 40 more minutes. Cool.

To make filling, cook egg yolks, ½ cup granulated sugar, lemon juice, and lemon zest in a saucepan over medium heat, stirring constantly, until thick. Remove from heat, and cool.

To make topping, whip cream and powdered sugar in a small bowl until stiff peaks form. Spread half of whipped cream on cooled crust; add filling and top with remaining half of whipped cream. Refrigerate.

Makes 6–8 servings.

 **Note:** This can be made a day ahead.

# Oatmeal-Coconut Cookies

**INGREDIENTS**

½ cup butter

½ cup shortening

1 cup granulated sugar

1 cup brown sugar

2 eggs, beaten

1 teaspoon vanilla extract

1 cup all-purpose flour

1½ teaspoons baking powder

1 teaspoon baking soda

½ teaspoon salt

2 cups dry oatmeal

2 cups coconut (or chocolate chips or raisins)

**DIRECTIONS**

Preheat oven to 350°.

In a large bowl, cream butter, shortening, and sugars. Mix in eggs and vanilla. In a medium bowl, sift together flour, baking powder, baking soda, and salt. Add flour mixture to creamed mixture, and mix. Stir in oatmeal and coconut. Form dough into balls, and place on baking sheets.

Bake for about 12 minutes or until brown.

Makes 4–5 dozen.

# Peanut Butter Cookies

**INGREDIENTS**

1 cup peanut butter

1 cup sugar

1 teaspoon baking powder

1 egg, beaten

**DIRECTIONS**

Preheat oven to 325°.

Mix together all ingredients well. Roll into balls the size of walnuts, and place on baking sheets.

Bake for about 10 minutes.

Makes about 3 dozen.

# Grandma's Ginger Cookies

## INGREDIENTS

¼ cup butter, softened

½ cup shortening

1 cup sugar

1 egg

1 teaspoon cinnamon

1 teaspoon cloves

1 teaspoon ginger

4 tablespoons molasses

2 teaspoons baking soda

2¼ cups all-purpose flour

Sugar

## DIRECTIONS

Preheat oven to 350°.

Cream butter, shortening, and sugar in a large bowl. Add egg and next 6 ingredients. Mix well. Chill dough. Roll dough into balls the size of a large marble. Dip into sugar, and place on baking sheets.

Bake for 10 minutes. If you want cracks on the top, sprinkle a few drops of water on each cookie before baking.

# Unbaked Cookies

## INGREDIENTS

2 cups carob chips or semi-sweet chocolate chips

1 cup peanut butter

1 (5-ounce) can chow mein noodles

Roasted Spanish peanuts or hulled sunflower seeds

## DIRECTIONS

Melt chips in a saucepan over low heat. Stir in peanut butter until well blended. Add chow mein noodles and nuts or seeds. Drop by teaspoonfuls onto wax paper. Let set to harden.

Makes 2–3 dozen.

# Moravian Sugar Cookies

## INGREDIENTS

½ cup butter, softened

1 cup sugar

1 teaspoon baking powder

1 teaspoon vanilla extract

¼ teaspoon salt

1 egg

1¼ cups all-purpose flour

## TOPPING

¼ cup sugar

2 teaspoons cinnamon

¼ cup finely chopped nuts (optional)

## DIRECTIONS

Preheat oven to 350°.

Combine butter, 1 cup sugar, baking powder, vanilla, and salt in a large bowl. Blend in egg and flour. Spread out half of dough on a well-greased baking sheet. Make a rectangle about 8x10 inches.

To make topping, combine ¼ cup sugar, cinnamon, and, if desired, nuts in a small bowl. Spread half of topping over dough.

Bake 12–15 minutes or until edges are golden brown. Cool 1 minute. Cut into squares or rectangles, and remove from pan while warm.

Repeat the process with remaining half of dough and topping.

Makes 2–3 dozen.

# Coconut Pudding Cookies

## INGREDIENTS

2 (3.4-ounce) packages instant coconut pudding mix

1½ cups butter

2½ cups all-purpose flour

## DIRECTIONS

Preheat oven to 350°.

Mix all ingredients together in a large bowl. Shape dough into balls and flatten; place on baking sheets.

Bake for 15 minutes.

Makes 6 dozen.

# Soda Cracker Cookies

## INGREDIENTS

35 soda crackers

1 cup brown sugar

1 cup butter

1 (12-ounce) package semi-sweet
  chocolate chips

½ cup chopped roasted walnuts

## DIRECTIONS

Preheat oven to 400°.

Line a 10x15-inch baking pan with aluminum foil.
Place crackers on the foil. Boil brown sugar and butter
in a saucepan for 3 minutes. Spread sugar mixture
over crackers.

Bake for 5 minutes. In the meantime, melt chocolate
chips in a saucepan over low heat. When crackers
have been removed from oven and the bubbling has
stopped (about 1 minute), spread melted chocolate on
top. Sprinkle with nuts. Pan may be put in freezer for
faster cooling. Cut or break into serving-size pieces.

Makes 35 servings.

# Monster Cookies

### INGREDIENTS

4 cups sugar

2 cups (1 pound) margarine

4½ cups (2 pounds) brown sugar

3 pounds (48 ounces) crunchy peanut butter

1 dozen eggs

1 tablespoon vanilla extract

8 teaspoons baking soda

18 cups (about 50 ounces) quick-cooking oatmeal

1 pound M&M's candies

1 pound semi-sweet chocolate chips

### DIRECTIONS

Preheat oven to 350°.

Combine sugar and next 6 ingredients in a large bowl. Mix well. Add oatmeal, candy, and chocolate chips. Mix well. Form dough into golf ball-size balls, and then flatten by hand. Place on baking sheets.

Bake 10–15 minutes, depending on size of cookies.

Makes 12 dozen.

**Note:** The source of this recipe is a mother who makes the dough at home, takes it to the cabin, and bakes a few dozen cookies at a time. They are large and filling. The dough keeps well in the refrigerator for quite a while. On your first try, you might want to make half the recipe.

# No-Bake Peanut Butter Drops

### INGREDIENTS

1 cup sugar

¼ cup margarine

¼ cup milk

1½ cups quick-cooking oatmeal

2½ tablespoons creamy peanut butter

¼ cup chopped roasted nuts

½ teaspoon vanilla extract

### DIRECTIONS

Combine sugar, margarine, and milk in a saucepan. Boil for 1 minute. Pour, while hot, over oatmeal and peanut butter in a large bowl. Add nuts and vanilla. Mix well. Drop by teaspoonfuls onto wax paper. Let stand until firm.

# Snickerdoodles

## INGREDIENTS

1 cup shortening, softened

1½ cups plus 3 tablespoons sugar, divided

2 eggs, beaten

2¾ cups all-purpose flour

2 teaspoons cream of tartar

1 teaspoon baking soda

½ teaspoon salt

1 tablespoon cinnamon

## DIRECTIONS

Preheat oven to 400°.

In a large bowl, cream shortening and 1½ cups sugar; stir in eggs. In a medium bowl, sift together flour, cream of tartar, baking soda, and salt. Mix flour mixture into creamed mixture. Chill.

Mix remaining 3 tablespoons sugar and cinnamon in a small bowl. Roll dough into walnut-size balls. Roll in sugar-cinnamon mixture. Place about 2 inches apart on ungreased baking sheets.

Bake 8–10 minutes. Cookies should be lightly browned but still soft.

Makes about 5 dozen.

# Nut Goody Bars

## INGREDIENTS

1 (12-ounce) package semi-sweet chocolate chips

1 (11-ounce) package butterscotch chips

1 cup peanut butter

1 (10-ounce) package miniature marshmallows

1 (16-ounce) can cocktail peanuts

## DIRECTIONS

Combine and melt chocolate chips and next two ingredients in a large saucepan over low heat. Cool slightly. Stir in marshmallows and peanuts. Spread mixture in a 9x13-inch baking pan. Cool. Cut into bars.

Makes 3 dozen.

# Sour Cream Raisin Bars

### INGREDIENTS

2 cups raisins

1 cup brown sugar

1 cup butter, softened

1⅓ cups quick-cooking oatmeal

1¾ cups all-purpose flour

1 teaspoon baking soda

3 egg yolks

1½ cups sour cream

1 cup granulated sugar

2½ tablespoons cornstarch

1 teaspoon vanilla extract

### DIRECTIONS

Preheat oven to 350°.

Cook and soften raisins in small amount of water in a saucepan for 10 minutes. Drain and cool. In a large bowl, cream brown sugar and butter. Mix in oatmeal, flour, and baking soda. Put half of oatmeal mixture in a 9x13-inch baking pan.

Bake for 7 minutes.

In a saucepan, mix egg yolks, sour cream, granulated sugar, and cornstarch. Simmer, stirring constantly. Add raisins and vanilla. Pour over baked crust. Crumble remaining half of oatmeal mixture over top. Bake 30 more minutes.

Makes 2–3 dozen.

# Mixed Nut Bars

### INGREDIENTS

1½ cups all-purpose flour

½ cup (1 stick) butter, softened

¾ cup brown sugar

Dash of salt

2 cups mixed nuts

½ cup light corn syrup

1 cup butterscotch chips

2 tablespoons butter

### DIRECTIONS

Preheat oven to 350°.

Mix and pat flour, ½ cup butter, brown sugar, and salt into an ungreased 9x13-inch baking pan.

Bake for 10 minutes. Sprinkle nuts over crust. Melt syrup, chips, and 2 tablespoons butter in a saucepan over low heat. Pour over nuts.

Bake for 10 more minutes. Cut into bars. Chill. Store in the refrigerator.

Makes 3 dozen.

# Mounds-Type Bars

## INGREDIENTS

2 cups crushed graham crackers

⅓ cup sugar

½ cup melted butter

2 cups shredded or flaked coconut

1 (14-ounce) can sweetened condensed milk

1 (12-ounce) bag semi-sweet chocolate chips

## DIRECTIONS

Preheat oven to 350°.

Mix crackers, sugar, and butter in a large bowl. Press mixture into a buttered 9x13-inch baking pan. Sprinkle coconut over crust. Pour milk over coconut.

Bake 15–20 minutes (top should be lightly brown). Melt chocolate chips in a saucepan over low heat. Spread over warm bars. Cool and cut.

Makes 2 dozen.


# Lemon Bars

## INGREDIENTS

2 cups plus 4 tablespoons all-purpose flour, divided

1 cup butter

1½ cups powdered sugar

4 eggs, slightly beaten

2 cups granulated sugar

1 teaspoon baking powder

6 tablespoons lemon juice

## GARNISH

Powdered sugar

## DIRECTIONS

Preheat oven to 350°.

Mix 2 cups flour, butter, and powdered sugar in a large bowl until crumbly. Pat mixture into a 9x13-inch baking pan.

Bake for 20 minutes. Cool.

Mix together eggs, granulated sugar, baking powder, lemon juice, and remaining 4 tablespoons flour. Pour over cooled crust.

Bake for 30 more minutes. Cool. Garnish, if desired.

Makes 2 dozen.

# Lazy Day Bars

### INGREDIENTS

½ cup butter

1½ cups graham cracker crumbs

1 (14-ounce) can sweetened condensed milk

¾ cup (6 ounces) semi-sweet chocolate chips

1 (3.5-ounce) can (1⅓ cups) flaked coconut

1 cup chopped nuts

### DIRECTIONS

Preheat oven to 350° (325° if using a glass baking dish).

Melt butter in a 9x13-inch baking pan in the oven. Sprinkle cracker crumbs over butter. Pour sweetened condensed milk evenly over crumbs. Top evenly with chocolate chips, coconut, and nuts; press down gently.

Bake 25–30 minutes or until lightly browned. Cool thoroughly before cutting. Store, loosely covered, at room temperature.

Makes 2 dozen.

# Corn Flake Bars

### INGREDIENTS

4 cups corn flakes

1 cup shredded or flaked coconut

⅓ cup slivered almonds

8 ounces marshmallows

⅓ cup butter

1 (7-ounce) milk chocolate candy bar

### DIRECTIONS

Preheat oven to 250°.

Combine corn flakes, coconut, and almonds in a 9x13-inch baking pan. Warm in the oven. Melt marshmallows and butter in a saucepan over low heat. Pour marshmallow mixture over corn flake mixture.

Melt chocolate bar in saucepan. Spread over top. Cool. Cut into squares.

Makes 2 dozen.

# Carrot Bars

### INGREDIENTS

1⅔ cups applesauce

3 eggs

⅓ cup vegetable oil

1 (15.25-ounce) box carrot cake mix

1 cup raisins

### TOPPING

1 can cream cheese frosting

½ cup chopped nuts (optional)

### DIRECTIONS

Preheat oven to 350°.

In a large bowl, blend applesauce, eggs, and oil. Mix for 1 minute at low speed. Add cake mix. Blend until moistened, and then beat for 2 minutes at medium speed. Stir in raisins. Spread into a lightly greased and floured 10x15-inch baking pan or in two 8- or 9-inch-square baking pans.

Bake 25–35 minutes or until a toothpick inserted in center comes out clean. Cool.

To make topping, spread frosting over bars. Sprinkle with nuts.

Makes 3 dozen.

 **Note:** These bars are best when refrigerated.

# Angel Food Bars

### INGREDIENTS

1 (16-ounce) box angel food cake mix

1 can lemon pie filling

1 cup flaked coconut

### GLAZE

2 cups powdered sugar, sifted

Juice from a small lemon

Milk

### DIRECTIONS

Preheat oven to 350°.

Combine dry cake mix and pie filling in a large bowl. Beat for about 5 minutes. Add coconut. Mix well. Pour into a lightly greased and floured jelly roll pan or 9x13-inch baking pan.

Bake 20–25 minutes.

To make glaze, mix powdered sugar and lemon juice together in a large bowl. Add enough milk (1 teaspoon at a time) to make a thin glaze. When bars are cool, spread glaze on top.

Makes 2 dozen.

# Graham Cracker Bars

## INGREDIENTS

Graham crackers

1 cup brown sugar

1 cup butter

½–1 cup chopped roasted nuts (walnuts, pecans, or sliced almonds)

1 cup milk chocolate chips (optional)

## DIRECTIONS

Preheat oven to 350°.

Line a 10x15-inch brownie pan with aluminum foil. Cover bottom of pan with graham crackers. Combine brown sugar and butter in a saucepan. Boil for 2 minutes. Pour over crackers. Sprinkle with nuts and, if desired, chocolate chips.

Bake for 5 minutes. Remove each cracker from pan and place on wax paper.

Makes 5–10 servings.

# Cream Cheese Bars

## INGREDIENTS

1 stick (½ cup) butter

1 (15.25-ounce) box yellow cake mix

3 eggs, divided

3½ cups (1 pound) powdered sugar

1 teaspoon vanilla extract

1 (8-ounce) package cream cheese, softened

## DIRECTIONS

Preheat oven to 300°.

Melt butter in a 9x13-inch baking pan in the oven. Swirl the melted butter around the pan to grease the bottom, and pour off the rest of the butter into a large bowl; add cake mix and 1 egg to bowl. Mix well. Pat batter into bottom of baking pan. On low speed, mix powdered sugar, vanilla, cream cheese, and remaining 2 eggs in a large bowl. Pour over batter.

Bake for 45–50 minutes or until top is golden brown.

Makes 2 dozen.

# Pumpkin Bars

## INGREDIENTS

2 cups all-purpose flour

2 teaspoons baking powder

1 teaspoon baking soda

½ teaspoon salt

2 teaspoons cinnamon

2 cups sugar

4 eggs, beaten

1 (15-ounce) can pumpkin

1 cup vegetable oil

### CREAM CHEESE FROSTING

3 ounces cream cheese, softened

6 tablespoons (¾ stick) butter

1 teaspoon milk

1 teaspoon vanilla extract

1¾ cups powdered sugar

## DIRECTIONS

Preheat oven to 350°.

Sift together flour and next 5 ingredients in a large bowl. Add eggs, pumpkin, and oil, and mix well.

Bake in a jelly roll pan for 25 minutes.

To make frosting, mix cream cheese and next 4 ingredients in a large bowl. Spread on cooled cake.

Makes 3 dozen.

# Salty Nut Bars

### INGREDIENTS

1½ cups all-purpose flour

¾ cup brown sugar

½ teaspoon salt

½ cup butter

1 (12-ounce) can salted mixed nuts
  or peanuts

### BUTTERSCOTCH TOPPING

1 (11-ounce) package butterscotch chips

½ cup light corn syrup

2 tablespoons butter

1 teaspoon vanilla extract

### DIRECTIONS

Preheat oven to 350°.

Mix flour and next 3 ingredients in a large bowl with a pastry blender. Pat flour mixture into a 9x13-inch buttered baking pan.

Bake for 10 minutes. Sprinkle nuts over baked layer.

To make topping, melt butterscotch and next 3 ingredients in a saucepan over low heat, stirring constantly. Spread over nuts.

Bake for 10 more minutes. Cut into squares while still a little warm.

Makes 2–3 dozen.

# Candy Bar Bars

### INGREDIENTS

4 cups oatmeal

1 cup brown sugar

⅔ cup butter

½ cup light corn syrup

2 teaspoons vanilla extract

1 cup semi-sweet chocolate chips

⅔ cup peanut butter

### DIRECTIONS

Preheat oven to 375°.

Mix oatmeal and brown sugar together in a large bowl. Melt butter and corn syrup in a saucepan over low heat. Add vanilla. Pour butter mixture into oatmeal mixture, and combine. Pat into the bottom of a 9x13-inch baking pan.

Bake for 10–12 minutes. Cool. Melt chocolate chips and peanut butter in a small saucepan over low heat. Spread on bars.

Makes 2–3 dozen.

# Speedy Little Devils

## INGREDIENTS

½ cup butter, melted

1 (15.25-ounce) devil's food cake mix

¾ cup creamy peanut butter

1 (7-ounce) jar marshmallow crème

## DIRECTIONS

Preheat oven to 350°.

Combine melted butter and dry cake mix in a large bowl. Reserve 1½ cups cake mixture for top crust. Pat remaining cake mixture into the bottom of an ungreased 9x13-inch baking pan. Combine peanut butter and marshmallow crème in a small bowl, and spread evenly in pan. Crumble 1½ cups reserved cake mixture over top.

Bake for 20 minutes. Cool.

Makes 3 dozen.

# Chocolate Scotcheroos

## INGREDIENTS

1 cup sugar

1 cup light corn syrup

1 cup peanut butter

6 cups Rice Krispies

¾ cup (6 ounces) semi-sweet chocolate chips

¾ cup (6 ounces) butterscotch chips

## DIRECTIONS

Combine sugar and syrup in a 3-quart saucepan. Cook over low heat, stirring constantly, just until mixture boils. Remove from heat. Blend in peanut butter. Stir in Rice Krispies. Press into bottom of a buttered 9x13-inch baking pan.

Melt chocolate and butterscotch chips in a double boiler or in a bowl over a pan of hot water. Spread on top. Cool and cut into bars.

Makes 30 bars.

# Marble Squares

## INGREDIENTS

1 (8-ounce) package cream cheese, softened

2⅓ cups sugar, divided

3 eggs, divided

2 cups all-purpose flour

½ cup butter

¾ cup water

1½ (1-ounce) squares unsweetened chocolate

½ cup sour cream

1 teaspoon baking soda

½ teaspoon salt

1 cup (8 ounces) semi-sweet chocolate chips

## DIRECTIONS

Preheat oven to 375°.

In a medium bowl, combine cream cheese and ⅓ cup sugar, mixing until well blended. Add 1 egg. Mix well, and set aside.

Combine flour and remaining 2 cups sugar in a large bowl. Bring butter, ¾ cup water, and chocolate squares to a boil in a saucepan. Mix into flour mixture. Add remaining 2 eggs, sour cream, baking soda, and salt. Mix well.

Pour batter into a lightly greased and floured jelly roll pan. Spoon cream cheese mixture over chocolate batter. Cut through batter with a knife several times to create a marble effect. Sprinkle with chocolate chips.

Bake 25–30 minutes. Cut into squares.

Makes 3 dozen.

# Caramel Layer Chocolate Squares

## INGREDIENTS

1 (11-ounce) bag caramels

1 (5-ounce) can evaporated milk, divided

1 (15.25-ounce) German chocolate cake mix

¾ cup butter, melted

1 cup chopped nuts

1 cup semi-sweet chocolate chips

## DIRECTIONS

Preheat oven to 350°.

In a saucepan over low heat, combine caramels and ⅓ cup milk (about half of the can). Cook, stirring until melted. Set aside. Lightly grease and flour a 9x13-inch baking pan. In a large bowl, combine cake mix, butter, remaining ⅓ cup milk, and nuts. Stir dough until it holds together. Press half of dough into bottom of prepared baking pan.

Bake for 6 minutes. Remove from oven. Sprinkle with chocolate chips. Spread caramel mixture over chips. Spread remaining half of dough over caramel mixture.

Bake 15–18 minutes. Cool in refrigerator for 30 minutes or overnight.

Makes 2–3 dozen.

# Caramel Krispies

## INGREDIENTS

1 (11-ounce) bag caramels

3 tablespoons water

5 cups Rice Krispies

1 cup peanuts

1 cup semi-sweet chocolate chips

1 cup butterscotch chips

## DIRECTIONS

Preheat oven to 200°.

Melt caramels with 3 tablespoons water in a saucepan over low heat. Stir frequently until sauce is smooth. Place cereal and peanuts in a large bowl; pour caramel mixture on top. Toss until well coated. With greased fingers, press mixture into a lightly greased 9x13-inch baking pan. Sprinkle chocolate and butterscotch chips on top.

Bake 5 minutes or until chips soften. Spread chips to create frosting. Cool at least 10 minutes before cutting.

Makes 2–3 dozen.

# Walnut Shortbread Squares

### INGREDIENTS

1 pound (2 cups) butter, softened

1 cup sugar

1 cup walnut pieces, coarsely ground

2 teaspoons vanilla extract

¼ teaspoon salt

4 cups all-purpose flour, sifted

### DIRECTIONS

Preheat oven to 325°.

Cream butter and sugar in a large bowl until light and fluffy. Beat walnuts, vanilla, and salt into creamed mixture. Add flour. Mix well. Spoon dough into a lightly greased 10x15-inch jelly roll pan; smooth it out, as the dough will not change shape as it bakes.

Bake for 45 minutes or until lightly browned. Cool in pan. Cut into bars. Store in a covered container.

Makes 75 (1-inch) bars.

 **Note:** These keep well for weeks.

# No-Bake Brownies

### INGREDIENTS

1 cup chopped walnuts

4 cups graham cracker crumbs

½ cup sifted powdered sugar

2 tablespoons instant coffee granules (optional)

1 (12-ounce) bag semi-sweet chocolate chips

1 cup evaporated milk

1 teaspoon vanilla extract

### DIRECTIONS

Combine walnuts, cracker crumbs, and powdered sugar in a large bowl. Heat coffee, if desired, chocolate chips, and milk in a saucepan over low heat. Stir constantly until smoothly blended. Remove from heat. Add vanilla.

Reserve ½ cup chocolate mixture. Mix remaining chocolate mixture into crumb mixture. Spread evenly in well-buttered 9x9-inch baking pan. Spread reserved ½ cup chocolate mixture over top.

Chill until ready to serve. Keep refrigerated.

Makes 32 brownies.

# Blond Brownies

## INGREDIENTS

5 tablespoons butter, softened

1 cup brown sugar

2 eggs

1 teaspoon vanilla extract

½ cup chopped walnuts

½ cup semi-sweet chocolate chips

1 cup sifted all-purpose flour

½ teaspoon baking powder

⅛ teaspoon baking soda

½ teaspoon salt

## DIRECTIONS

Preheat oven to 350°.

Cream butter and brown sugar in a large bowl. Add eggs and next 7 ingredients. Mix well. Pour into a lightly greased and floured 9x9-inch baking pan.

Bake 20–25 minutes. (For a double recipe, use a 9x13-inch pan, and bake for 30 minutes.)

Makes 18 brownies.

# Cream Cheese Brownies

## BROWNIE LAYER

1 (18.2-ounce) package chocolate brownie mix

1 teaspoon almond extract

## CREAM CHEESE LAYER

4 tablespoons (½ stick) butter, softened

1 8-ounce package cream cheese

1½ cups sugar

2 eggs

2 tablespoons all-purpose flour

1 teaspoon vanilla extract

## DIRECTIONS

Preheat oven to 350°.

To make cream cheese layer, cream butter and cream cheese in a large bowl. Blend in sugar and next 3 ingredients; spread over brownie layer. Swirl a knife through the layers to make a zigzag pattern.

To make cream cheese layer, cream butter and cream cheese in a large bowl. Blend in sugar and next 3 ingredients, and spread on top of brownie layer. Zigzag cream cheese mixture through brownie mixture, using a knife or fork.

Bake for 35 minutes.

Makes 2–3 dozen.

# Hershey's Chocolate Brownies

## INGREDIENTS

½ cup (1 stick) butter, softened

1 cup sugar

1½ cups Hershey's syrup

1 cup all-purpose flour

4 eggs

½ teaspoon salt

1 teaspoon vanilla extract

¾ cup chopped nuts

## FROSTING

1 cup sugar

4 tablespoons (½ stick) butter

¼ cup milk

½ cup semi-sweet chocolate chips

## DIRECTIONS

Preheat oven to 350°.

Cream ½ cup butter and 1 cup sugar in a large bowl. Add syrup and next 5 ingredients. Mix well for about 4 minutes. Spread batter on a 10x15-inch jelly roll pan.

Bake for 20 minutes or until done.

To make frosting, boil 1 cup sugar, 4 tablespoons butter, and milk in a saucepan for 1 minute. Remove from heat. Add chocolate chips. Stir until smooth. Immediately spread on brownies.

Makes 2–3 dozen.

# Kay's Chocolate Fudge

## INGREDIENTS

2 cups sugar

1 (5-ounce) can evaporated milk

10 regular-size marshmallows

¾ cup (6 ounces) semi-sweet chocolate chips

½ cup (1 stick) butter, cut up

1 teaspoon vanilla extract

## DIRECTIONS

Combine sugar, milk, and marshmallows in a heavy saucepan. Bring to a boil, stirring constantly. Place chocolate chips, butter, and vanilla in a medium bowl; stir in sugar mixture. Pour into a 9x9-inch baking pan. Cool. Cut into pieces, and refrigerate.

Makes 81 pieces.

# Chocolate Candies

## INGREDIENTS

2 squares unsweetened baking chocolate

1 (5-ounce) can sweetened condensed milk

Dash of salt

1 teaspoon vanilla extract

Crushed roasted nuts and/or flaked coconut

## DIRECTIONS

Mix chocolate, milk, and salt together in a saucepan. Stir over low heat until thick. Add vanilla, and let cool somewhat, stirring occasionally.

Before it cools completely, form into small balls, and roll in nuts or coconut. Refrigerate.

Makes 1–2 dozen.

# Beverages

# Fruit Crush

## INGREDIENTS

3 cups water

2 cups sugar

1 (46-ounce) can pineapple juice

1½ cups orange juice

¼ cup lemon juice

3 ripe bananas, mashed

1½ (2-liter) bottles ginger ale or sparkling
water, chilled

## DIRECTIONS

In a large soup pot, mix 3 cups water and sugar.
Bring to a boil. Remove from heat. Stir in pineapple,
orange, and lemon juices and mashed bananas.
(Bananas can be mashed in a blender or a food
processor, with a small amount of juice.) Pour
mixture into 4 ice cube freezer trays. Freeze until
firm. When frozen, cubes can be put into zip-top
plastic bags for easy cooler storage or transport.

To serve, take from freezer about 15 minutes before
serving. Break up enough cubes to fill glasses ⅓ full
of fruit crush. Fill remainder of glass with ginger ale
or sparkling water. Stir.

Makes 6 quarts or 24 servings.


# Cranberry Punch

## INGREDIENTS

1 quart (32 ounces) cranberry juice cocktail,
chilled

2 cups pineapple juice, chilled

1½ cups sugar

1 (2-liter) bottle ginger ale, chilled

## DIRECTIONS

Combine cranberry and pineapple juices with sugar.
Just before serving, add ice cubes and ginger ale.

Makes 28 servings.

# Mock Champagne

### INGREDIENTS

Apple cider or juice

Pineapple juice

Ginger ale

### DIRECTIONS

Combine equal parts apple and pineapple juices in a pitcher. Pour over ice in glasses, and top with ginger ale just before serving.

# Cranberry Slush

### INGREDIENTS

1 quart (32 ounces) cranberry juice cocktail

1 (12-ounce) container frozen lemonade

12 ounces (1½ cups) bourbon

### DIRECTIONS

Mix all ingredients in a 1-gallon plastic container, such as an ice cream pail. Freeze. Remove from freezer when ready to use.

# Kool-Aid Punch for the Lake Crowd

### INGREDIENTS

1 envelope unsweetened black cherry Kool-Aid

1 envelope unsweetened strawberry Kool-Aid

3 quarts water

2 cups sugar

1 (6-ounce) can frozen orange juice

1 (6-ounce) can frozen lemonade

1 quart ginger ale

### DIRECTIONS

Mix together Kool-Aid, 3 quarts water, and next 3 ingredients in a large punch bowl. Stir in ginger ale just before serving.

Makes 48 servings.

# Orange Julia

### INGREDIENTS

½ (12-ounce) container frozen orange juice

1 cup milk

1 cup water

¼–½ cup sugar

1 teaspoon vanilla extract

10 ice cubes

### DIRECTIONS

Mix orange juice and next 4 ingredients in a blender at low speed, gradually adding ice cubes. Blend until completely smooth.

Makes 4 servings.

# Easiest Lemonade

### INGREDIENTS
Juice of 1 large lemon

½ cup sugar

1 quart water

### DIRECTIONS
Mix. Chill. Serve over ice cubes.

# Root Beer Float

### INGREDIENTS
Vanilla ice cream

Root beer

### DIRECTIONS
Place ice cream in a tall glass, and fill with root beer.

# Ginger Tea

### INGREDIENTS

3 tea bags

1 cup boiling water

Juice of 2 oranges

Juice of 2 lemons

½ cup sugar

1 (1-liter) bottle ginger ale, chilled

### DIRECTIONS

Make a cup of strong tea by putting 3 tea bags into 1 cup boiling water in a saucepan; brew for 5 minutes. Remove tea bags. Mix with orange and lemon juices and sugar.

Chill. Just before serving, add ginger ale.

Makes 5 (8-ounce) servings.

# Sun Tea

### INGREDIENTS

4 tea bags

### DIRECTIONS

Fill a 2-quart glass jar with cold water. Put 4 tea bags in jar, with tags hanging on outside. Screw on cover. Put out in the sun for 4 to 6 hours. Chill and serve over ice.

# Margie's Mist

## INGREDIENTS

10 ounces water

1¼ cups sugar

14 ounces vodka

6 heaping tablespoons Ovaltine

Drop of rum extract

1 pint whipping cream

## DIRECTIONS

Simmer 10 ounces water and sugar in a saucepan. Cool. Stir in vodka and next 3 ingredients. Transfer to a 2-quart container. Store in refrigerator. Shake well before serving.


# Hot Buttered Rum Mix

## INGREDIENTS

½ cup (1 stick) butter, softened

1 pound dark brown sugar

¼ teaspoon cinnamon

¼ teaspoon nutmeg

¼ teaspoon cloves

Rum

## GARNISHES

Cinnamon sticks, lemon slices

## DIRECTIONS

Cream butter and sugar in a large bowl. Add cinnamon, nutmeg, and cloves. Mix well. Store in a covered container in the refrigerator.

To serve, put 1 heaping tablespoon mixture in a cup. Add 1½ ounces dark rum. Fill with boiling water. Garnish, if desired.

Makes 12–14 servings.

*Potpourri*

# Best Ever Fudge Sauce

## INGREDIENTS

¾ cup (6-ounces) semi-sweet chocolate chips

½ cup butter

2 cups powdered sugar, sifted

1⅓ cups evaporated milk

1 teaspoon vanilla extract

Vanilla ice cream

## DIRECTIONS

Melt chocolate and butter in a medium saucepan. Remove from heat. Add sugar and milk. Blend. Bring to a boil, stirring constantly. Cook and stir for about 8 minutes. Add vanilla.

Serve warm over ice cream.

 **Note:** Store in a covered container in the refrigerator.

# Fabulous Fudge Sauce

## INGREDIENTS

1 (12-ounce) package semi-sweet chocolate chips

1 cup miniature marshmallows

1 (14-ounce) can sweetened condensed milk

½ cup milk

1 teaspoon vanilla extract

Vanilla ice cream

## DIRECTIONS

Combine chocolate chips and the next 4 ingredients in a large saucepan. Heat slowly over low heat, until chips and marshmallows are melted. Stir occasionally.

Cool and refrigerate. Reheat before serving over ice cream.

Makes 15–20 servings.

# Butterscotch Sauce

## INGREDIENTS

1 pound dark brown sugar

1 cup sugar

1 cup half-and-half

1 stick butter

2 teaspoons vanilla extract

## DIRECTIONS

Combine all ingredients in the top of a double boiler. Cook slowly until thick.

Makes 12 servings.

 **Note:** Do not freeze. It keeps up to 3 weeks in the refrigerator.


# Cinnamon Blueberry Sauce

## INGREDIENTS

½ cup sugar

4 teaspoons cornstarch

½ teaspoon lemon zest

¼ teaspoon cinnamon

Dash of salt

⅔ cup water

1 (10-ounce) package frozen blueberries, thawed and divided

1 teaspoon fresh lemon juice

## DIRECTIONS

In a small bowl, combine sugar, cornstarch, lemon zest, cinnamon, and salt. Set aside.

In a medium saucepan, combine ⅔ cup water and ½ cup blueberries. Bring to a boil and mash berries. Add sugar mixture; cook and stir until sauce thickens and bubbles. Add remaining blueberries and lemon juice. Simmer 3–5 minutes.

Makes 2 cups.

 **Note:** Serve warm on waffles, pancakes, or French toast.

# Strawberry Topping for Pancakes or French Toast

## INGREDIENTS

1 (8-ounce) package cream cheese, softened

1 stick butter

½–¾ cup powdered sugar

1 teaspoon vanilla extract

8 large strawberries, mashed

## DIRECTIONS

Combine all ingredients. Mix well. Store in the refrigerator.

# Strawberry or Raspberry Jam for Freezer

## INGREDIENTS

3 cups fresh berries

5 cups sugar

1 (1.75-ounce) package powdered pectin

1 cup water

## DIRECTIONS

Wash and hull berries. Mash in a large bowl. Add sugar. Mix well. Let stand for about 15 minutes, stirring occasionally.

Dissolve pectin in 1 cup water in a saucepan, and boil for 1 minute. Add mixture to fruit. Stir for 2 minutes. Pour into freezer containers, cover, and let stand until jelled. Freeze.

**Note:** This will also keep well in the refrigerator for 1 month. May also be used as a topping for ice cream or pound cake.

# Fresh Strawberry Topping

**DIRECTIONS**

Clean and cut up fresh strawberries. Sprinkle lightly with sugar, until it suits your taste of sweetness. Chill for several hours or overnight.

Use as a topping for ice cream, shortcake, pound cake, angel food cake, pancakes, etc. You may choose to use it in combination with slightly sweetened whipped cream.

# Rhubarb Freezer Jam

**INGREDIENTS**

2 cups chopped rhubarb

1 cup sugar

1 (3-ounce) package strawberry gelatin mix

1 (8-ounce) can crushed pineapple, undrained

**DIRECTIONS**

Cook rhubarb and sugar in a saucepan until soft. Add gelatin mix, pineapple, and pineapple juice.

Bring to a boil. Simmer for 15 minutes. Pour into sterilized jars. Freeze.

# Orange Sauce for Wild Game

### INGREDIENTS
1 cup orange marmalade

½ cup orange juice

2 tablespoons freshly grated orange peel

2 tablespoons orange-flavored liqueur

### DIRECTIONS
Combine all ingredients in a small saucepan.

Heat over low heat, stirring until smooth.

# Parmesan Croutons

### INGREDIENTS
8 slices bread

¼ cup butter, melted

¼ cup grated Parmesan cheese

### DIRECTIONS
Preheat oven to 375°.

Remove crusts and cube bread. Toss with melted butter and Parmesan cheese in a large bowl. Place on a baking sheet.

Bake for about 10 minutes. When cool, store in airtight container.

# Barbecue Sauce

**INGREDIENTS**

3 garlic cloves

2 tablespoons butter

1 cup ketchup

¼ cup water

2 tablespoons brown sugar

2 teaspoons liquid smoke

1 tablespoon Worcestershire sauce

½ teaspoon salt

¼ teaspoon pepper

**DIRECTIONS**

Slice garlic cloves; brown in butter in a skillet over medium heat. Discard garlic. Stir in ketchup and next 6 ingredients. Simmer for 10 minutes.

Makes 1½ cups.

# Best Barbecue Sauce

**INGREDIENTS**

1 medium onion, chopped

5 tablespoons butter, melted

¾ cup brown sugar

12 ounces mustard

2 ounces (¼ cup) liquid smoke

1 tablespoon garlic powder

1 (32-ounce) bottle ketchup

½ cup Worcestershire sauce

⅓ cup lemon juice

2½ cups water

**DIRECTIONS**

Sauté onion in butter in a large saucepan over medium heat. Add brown sugar. Mix well. Add mustard and next 6 ingredients. Bring to a boil, and simmer for 30 minutes, stirring occasionally.

Makes 2½ quarts.

 **Note:** Store in refrigerator. It keeps well for a long time. Use on hamburgers, ribs, chicken, brisket, steak, and more.

# Index

## CONTRIBUTORS OF RECIPES

Peggy Alberg

Esther Allen

Ginny Anderson

Lois Anderson

Gail Barduson

Dorothy Boen

Betty Bordwell

Lola Brubacher

Olga Brubacher

Sara Brubacher

Faye Burke

Kay Burke

Sandy Burke

Mildred Burke

Hazel Cannon

Janet Carlson

Billie Cashman

Mary Choinere

Marge Coppins

Jo Crisman

Liz Cullen

Nancy Damerow

Bette Dedon

Terry Dee

Rosemary Dineen

Kathy Dirks

Eleanor Donaghy

Marie Edstrom

Georgiana Ehrlichmann

Lynn Empanger

Barb Engmark

Ole Enli

Miriam Erdahl

Char Erickson

Mary Ernst

Marian Ertl

Joyce Fargo

Kitty Felion

Michelle Felion

Margaret Feudner

Bonnie Fischer

Gerry Fleming

Trudy Forster

Bev Gerber

Barb Graf

Lucy Grams

Judy Grothe

Donna Gustafson

Francis Gustafson

Evy Hagen

Laurie Halter

Marian Hart

Jean Helgeson

Ruth Hopperstad

Gladys Jacobson

Howard Jacobson

Norma Jacobson

Larry Jeffery

Carol Johnson

Helen Johnson

Louise Jones

Betty Keunzli

Betty Kidder

Mice Kilby

Joe Knoblauch

Lorraine Knoblauch

LuAnne Knoblauch

Mary Knoblauch

Carolyn Krautkremer

Elaine Krenik

Carolyn Latz

Marilyn Lehman

Nola Lockwood

Helene Lohmann

Audrey Lommen

Sharon Magnuson

Ann Mark

Doris Maser

Elaine May

Ann McCormick

Michael McCuddin

Carol Mereness

Janine Merrick

Virginia Merrick

Kathy Mimnaugh

Alice Mol

Mona Nagel

Barb Nelson

Mary Nelson

Bernice Ness

Mary Niemann

Audrey Novak

Ruth Novotny

Marlene Olseth

Nancy Olseth

Clara Olson

Ginger Overbye

Ethel Payne

Bob Paul

Ruby Perkins

Kay Peterson

Lucille Petrak

Carol Pohle

June Raarup

Diane Rabe

Susie Redpath

Lea Rae Reese

Carolyn Ring

Jo Roseborough

Joan Ryberg

Lynne Segal

Anne Senn

Pat Shearer

Bobbie Shoemaker

Nikki Sindt

Betsy Skjervold

Dianne E. Smith

Mary Ellen Solberg

Judy Sotebeer Sharon

Stefan Mary Straka

Gail Swalve

Pat Tagader

Irene Tanglen

Bev Thurn

Vi Towley

Carol Tveit

Shirley Velner

Lorraine Wagner

Dawn Wanous

Diana Waterbury

Perry Wegleitner

Sue Weinstein

Dorothy Welch

Carol Wentzlaff

Aileen Wigginton

Mary Lou Williams

Peg Wilhoit

Carol Witsoe

# About the Authors

Margie Knoblauch was a Minnesota native who lived in the Minnetonka-Hopkins area of the Twin Cities. A wife and the mother of six children, she spent her summers at the family's log cabin, "Knobby Pines," near Park Rapids, Minnesota.

Margie was a University of Minnesota home economics graduate with a degree in institutional management, and worked as a home economist for Northern States Power Company and as a representative of Admiral Corporation. She was a member of Home Economics in Homemaking, a group of home economics graduates, and was involved in the marketing of a cookbook for that group.

Margie's family has been involved in several food-and-beverage establishments in Minnesota, including the Hopkins House and Breezy Point Resort.

---

Mary Brubacher, a resident of Hopkins, Minnesota, has had a long-time interest in collecting recipes and cookbooks and preparing special foods. She has also helped produce a cookbook for a women's group in Hopkins.

A wife and the mother of three daughters, Mary has been a "cabin person" at Little Hubert Lake, near Nisswa, Minnesota. She is a graduate of Hamline University, with a bachelor's degree in nursing, and was a school nurse in the Hopkins School District.